PEARLS OF WISDOM & POWER

Life Changing Lessons for Spiritual Advancement

WRITTEN BY:

MICHELLE DORNOR

COPYRIGHT

Printed in the United States of America

First Printing, 2023

Dornor Consulting Publishing

Cheyenne, Wyoming

http://dornorconsulting.services

Dedication

I want to dedicate this book to my biggest cheerleader, my husband Victor. If you never told me to get on Clubhouse and use my voice, this book probably would not exist. I love you.

Why I wrote this book

I wrote this book because it was time to write a nonfiction book. Now my listeners and people all around the world can refer to the selection of 12 life lessons again and again from the first full year of the Pearls of Wisdom and Power Tuesday Inspiration room.

This book was written in research, note taking form. While I did fill in and elaborate for better understanding in some parts, I left my notes from the shows as is in their integrity. Enjoy my process.

MY ASK

My hope is that the words contained herein will encourage your spirit to pursue your highest good and purpose. If the words herein have touched you in some way please leave a positive review & share on your social media pages with the hashtag:

#pearlsofwisdomandpower

With Love, Michelle

TABLE OF CONTENTS

Photo courtesy of Pexels.com by Brett Jordan

THE STORY OF PEARLS OF WISDOM & POWER

It all started with my husband calling me "The Voice" one night when he heard me speaking on a social platform in a room full of people. He had told me about an app called Clubhouse a few months before that night. He told me that I should join it and start a room sharing my wisdom and knowledge. At that time, I had thought who would come listen to me as I felt I had failed miserably as I stared into a camera for months on Facebook Live talking to no one every Sunday night.

Nevertheless, I joined via an invite from my childhood friend Sherrita. I thought it wouldn't hurt to check it out. I had some ups and downs but, eventually I found success. I opened a room titled Abena Grand Rising with Prophetess Michelle on Clubhouse and the Wisdom app. I chose Abena because in the Akan language, it means a female who is Tuesday born and I am Tuesday born. Abena women are to themselves but if you try them you will find out that they possess a little fire in them! Tuesday in Astrology is ruled by Mars, which is known as the God of War so it makes sense that women born on Tuesday would have a little spunk in their spirit. I was supposed to have a guest come help me, but they backed out on me at the literal last minute, and I was determined to not let that stop me, so I held the room by myself. It's so crazy because 5 minutes before the room started the guest said they will be in the audience to support me. I would rather they not. It was like a thorn in my side seeing someone who offered help when I didn't ask for it back out and then show up, but I ignored my feelings and held my very first room with a person who let me down sit in the very small audience. Boy was I getting a lesson in patience and overlooking stuff, haha!

I got over that fiasco of a first room and continued full speed ahead. I was getting traction on the Wisdom app, and NO ONE would show up for the Clubhouse room, not even allllllll the people who said oh yeah Michelle, you should open a room I will be there! Y'all should hear me laughing right now but back then I was mad enough to cry and tide, not tired, tide of folks pretending and lying to me because nan one of them showed up EVER, hahaha!

I remember one room titled *Walking in your Design: An Esoteric Study* only had two people in it the entire time: My husband and me! I was the speaker and he stayed and listened for the whole hour and twenty-five minutes message I gave. Gratitude to my husband for being my biggest supporter since day one! He would come home and ask me how did my room go and I would bust out in tears and tell him no one showed up. I felt like quitting after months of talking to an empty screen. He told me not to give up. That's when I started taking astrology classes and one of my classmates heard I was doing a room on clubhouse, and she faithfully showed up every single week just to listen to me talk. I couldn't believe it. She restored my faith in people and healed my heart by doing that. You know who you are. Thank you.

I went from just my husband and I to my husband and I and my Astrology classmate to now seeing anywhere from 100 to 200+ people come thru the space every week for the rest of the year! I have also acquired several paying recurring clients for my Clarity sessions and numerous readings. I'm sharing this for that person reading this who is about to give up on your dream because nothing is happening for you yet. I started that room in January and it wasn't till May which is five months later of doing weekly room that I started getting a hand full of people staying and listening to the entire message! Don't you DARE throw in the towel! As the old church folks would tell you, God is not done with you yet! If you have a dream in your heart and you can't stop thinking about it, don't you EVER EVER give up!!!!

I started the Abena room on a Sunday afternoon then my schedule changed at work, and I switched it to Tuesday morning. I had the Prophetess title in it, and I didn't want to use titles, so I sat with Spirit until I came up with Pearls of Wisdom and Power because I wear pearls a lot. The name checked out numerically and the rest is herstory. I went from zero members to two members (my husband and my classmate, lol) to 100 members and currently sitting at 927 members. You never know what will happen if you just keep going. Being a Vigo Sun in both tropical and sidereal systems, I have perfectionist tendencies and strive for excellence in everything that I do so I do not call what I have accomplished so far as success. While I do celebrate my wins along the way, I know there is still more work to do and more platforms to conquer.

Please Enjoy the 12 lessons from the Tuesday Inspiration Talk Show along with 12 winning formulas for life and 12 Pearls of Wisdom & Power "moments". My hope is that you will find the joy, strength and courage to "make the rest of your life, the best of your life" in the words of one of my silent mentors, Dr. Eric Thomas. This book was written with my audience in mind. I appreciate and love you all.

<u>**January 9th, 2022: My first Clubhouse room**</u>

<u>**Transform Chaos Into Power: My Story/ 1 hour 20 min**</u>

The process of transformation

Transformation only comes by way of sitting in the dark long enough to come to the light. So let's look at two definitions of the words light and dark from a Google search.

Light definition

The natural agent that stimulates sight and makes things visible. a source of illumination. understanding of a problem or mystery; enlightenment. Old English German and Indo-European root meaning white, lung ⍰, and lessen the weight of.

Isn't it true when we feel a relief we take a deep breath 😮 💨 a breath of fresh air... So, light is a fresh breath of air.

Dark definition

Understanding of a problem or mystery; enlightenment. hidden from knowledge; mysterious. ignorant; unenlightened. the absence of light in a place. in a state of ignorance about something. German root that means conceal.

Doesn't our breathing change when we don't know what's going on? Doesn't it become shallow and constricted? We freeze, we lock up? We must learn to use our white light, our lungs, and BREATHE 🧖🏽 thru chaos! Doing so will "lighten the load" and you will be able to see your way through the dark.

Butterflies go through a process called metamorphosis. It is just another fancy way of saying change. Transformation is also change. Let's look at the Hebrew definition and root meaning of the word change.

Definition of change in Hebrew

שָׁנָה **shânâh,** shaw-naw'; a primitive root; to fold, i.e. duplicate (literally or figuratively); by implication, to transmute (transitive or intransitive):—do (speak, strike) again, alter, double, (be given to) change, disguise, (be) diverse, pervert, prefer, repeat, return, do the second time.

When something changes, doesn't it alter or pervert the way the thing look beforehand? Let's look at the definition for pervert. Stay with me, Im going somewhere.

Pervert
alter (something) from its original course, meaning, or state to a distortion or corruption of what was first intended. late Middle English (as a verb): from Old French *pervertir*, from Latin *pervertere*, from *per-* 'thoroughly, to ill effect' + *vertere* 'to turn.' The current noun sense dates from the late 19th century.

Now let's look at the Greek definition transform.

Transform Greek definition

μετασχηματίζω **metaschēmatízō,** met-askh-ay-mat-id'-zo; to transfigure or disguise; figuratively, to apply (by accommodation):—transfer, transform (self). μετά **metá,** met-ah'; a primary preposition (often used adverbially); properly, denoting accompaniment; "amid" (local or causal); modified variously according to the case (genitive association, or accusative succession) with which it is joined. With, after, behind.

So when it comes to transformation, the process is quite chaotic! You have someone who feels trapped in the dark, needs to take deep breaths to handle the dark. They start going through the process of change and they don't recognize themselves anymore as what they are going through is perverting their image into something they no longer recognize. And this new person emerging looks like a disguise on all fronts!

Transformation is not some easy carefree shooting the breeze kind of thing! You will never be the same again once you are done!

We transform by connecting...

Its in connecting that we learn to truly detach
We were born to connect
For true transformation to take place we must accept that we drew these experiences to us
Stop trying to be morally good

I always tried to maintain a certain image of the good person. Trying to be a goody two shoes at all times kept me from transforming into the person I was destined to be. A truly upright person knows there is a time for everything. It includes knowing when to say yes and when to practice tough love and tell someone no.

We stay stuck because...

We don't want to be the one to judge because we know what that feels like.

We want to be the good person who helps everyone.

You can't save the world!
When you continue to do that, you will interrupt that person's transformation and reap karma from imposing your will on another. Yes you are getting burned because you keep sticking your nose in something that is none of your business! You break spiritual law when you try to rescue people.
Stop interrupting peoples karma and you will stop getting burned.

Empty people devoid of light are attracted to your light like the moth. Wicked people are empty and wicked just means twisted. So these people that come to you for help are twisted in their thinking and way of being. They are attracted to the light... the moon... That's you!
They are chasing people instead of chasing the "Lord their God"! We will find out in a second what that means when I break it down.
They are not in tune, so they are disoriented and gravitate to you instead of going within to spirit!
They are trying to get from people what they should be getting from "God"...
They can't get it from Source because it's their karma, so they use dubious means

But they will be the one getting burned... and you need to stay out the way!

Transformation is like Kabbalah
Kabbalah is a Hebrew word which means received... you have to receive the lesson the chaos has presented to transform yourself. The Universe is always trying to get our attention by the things we go through.

You cannot study transformation. You cannot even help someone else transform. You must experience it for yourself.

You can study it all you want but you wont truly get it until you experience it...

SOME THINGS CAN ONLY BE EXPERIENCED

You must Let go COMPLETELY

Don't be mad at your experiences you needed them to elevate
You need the chaos, the lessons to elevate

Just as Heru in Kemetic philosophy you can only become a master of this world by connecting thru spirit by WALKING through and experiencing this realm ... this is about letting go and receiving the lessons of transformation. This is how you bring heaven to earth and is what will allow you to live here in bliss.

The stars were birthed from chaos
People will be drawn to your light... and your darkness
You can change your trajectory
What got you here won't get you there
Its for your mastery!

Your intuition is your best friend during transformation.
God said when you don't obey me all these things will overtake you! What will overtake you? All the strain and stress of transformation. Do you know who God is??? God is your intuition!!! That is the Lord your God!
When you don't listen to your intuition, you are disobeying the voice of the Lord your God!

In Torah, Satan is an agent of the Most High! An agent used to teach you a life lesson just like Saturn in Astrology. Use the lessons of the dark to come to light. This is how you transform!

Let's look at change one more time in the Hebrew.

Definition of change in Hebrew

שָׁנָה **shânâh,** shaw-naw'; a primitive root; to fold, i.e. duplicate (literally or figuratively); by implication, to transmute (transitive or intransitive):—do (speak, strike) again, alter, double, (be given to) change, disguise, (be) diverse, pervert, prefer, repeat, return, **do the second time**.

Problems are a chance to do it again... The only reason why problems exist is because something was not done right the first time... problems are a chance for **redemption**.

Problems only exist and persist because you are not listening to your intuition. Now you are being forced to listen for not honoring spirit! Ouch!

Look at the word Pervert again!

Pervert
alter (something) from its original course, meaning, or state to a distortion or corruption of what was first intended. late Middle English (as a verb): from Old French *pervertir*, from Latin *pervertere*, from *per-* 'thoroughly, to ill effect' + *vertere* 'to turn.' The current noun sense dates from the late 19th century.

You have to alter the problem into a lesson! You can't just leave it or try to run from it! Face it and look for the lesson or the opportunity or both.

You have the power to alter the chaos in your life by turning it completely around from its opposite effect... but how?

Let's look at a few definitions and I will bring it all together for you.

Transitive
able to take a direct object. mid 16th century (in the sense 'transitory'): from late Latin *transitivus*, from *transit-* 'gone across' (see transit).

Intransitive
not taking a direct object, n grammar, an intransitive verb does not allow a direct object. This is distinct from a transitive verb, which takes one or more objects. The verb property is called transitivity. Intransitive verbs are often identified as those that cannot be followed by who or what.

Transform Greek definition

μετασχηματίζω **metaschēmatízō,** met-askh-ay-mat-id'-zo; to transfigure or disguise; figuratively, to apply (by accommodation):—transfer, transform (self). μετά **metá,** met-ah'; a primary preposition (often used adverbially); properly, denoting accompaniment; "amid" (local or causal); modified variously according to the case (genitive association, or accusative succession) with which it is joined. With, after, behind. σχῆμα **schēma,** skhay'-mah; a figure (as a mode or circumstance), i.e. (by implication) external condition. to hold oneself to a thing, to lay hold of a thing, to adhere or cling to, to be closely joined to a person or a thing!

What does all this mean Michelle???

You have to get intimate WITH the chaos, you have to go AFTER IT by getting behind it. Supporting the chaos by sitting with it is supporting and ushering in your transformation!

Understand the light works with the dark
Get with it after it and behind it
To transmute you have to accept as well as reject.
First step is to identify what exactly it is
Can't transmute what you can't identify
Be honest about how it feels and what it looks like
Accept what is happening to you
Accept what is happening through you
Accept what others are doing to you and transmute it by not trying to control it
Reject the urge to control it
That means let go! This is the rejection part!

Reject the urge to fight!
The hard part is to sit with it by looking for the lesson!
When you are willing to sit with it and be introspective that is the power to transmute or change the situation!
Now rename it! This is transmutation!

By doing this you pervert the chaos, you disguise it to look like something else because it is… it is not a problem, it is a lesson and a chance to elevate! Once you learn the lesson, the chaos of the situation will disappear and you will be a new person, a better person regardless of the outcome.

The Winning Formula For Transformation

Get well acquainted with things not going your way
Do it afraid
Reveal it, you can't heal what you wont reveal
Follow the Lord YOUR God, that's your intuition!
The old you will and must die so Surrender control
Pervert the chaos… make it your punk lol

Pearl of Wisdom & Power Moment

Photo courtesy of Pexels.com by Isil Agc

"MAKE A MESS"

Just like that picture above, transformation can be messy. So go ahead... make a mess. You are going to have bumps in the road, detours, people canceling on you and making promises they can't keep and the like. You are going to laugh, cry, and feel like you want to pull your hair out. This is all a part of the process of transformation. You can clean up after you become a new person.

February 20, 2022

The Sacral: Your Seat of Power, 1 hour 2 minutes

WHAT IS THE SACRAL?

https://jamanetwork.com/journals/jama/article-abstract/365627

"The os sacrum (sacred bone) was so named by the Romans as a direct translation from the older Greek hieron osteon. Explanations of the attribute "sacred" or "holy" in the past have included misinterpretation of the Greek word hieron, use of the bone in sacrificial rites, the role of the bone in protecting the genitalia (themselves considered sacred), and the necessity for the intactness of this bone as a nidus for resurrection at the Day of Judgment. A more plausible explanation may be that the holiness of the sacral bone was an attribute borrowed from the ancient Egyptians, who considered this bone sacred to Osiris, the god of resurrection and of agriculture. It is the second chakra from the root, color orange. It is located below the belly button and encompasses the sex organs, the kidneys, the sacrum bone and the sacral canal and nerves. The Sanskrit name [for the sacral chakra] is Svadhisthana," The symbol of the sacral chakra is a moon crescent, which represents the relationship between the tides of water and the phases of the moon." Located in the ninth sphere of the tree of life which resembles the vagus nerve, it is governed by Cancer ♋ which is governed by the Moon. Scorpio also rules the reproductive organs, so it is governed by Mars and Pluto as well with initiation and transformative power. In Sanskrit, Svadihsthana means "where your being is established." Sva means self and the rest of the letters mean dwelling place or seat. It is the seat of your self! It contains who you are at your core!" (From article link above Internet search)

WHAT DOES THE SACRAL DO?

Seat of our experiences, our emotions which is the foundation
Associated with Cancer which is governed by the Moon

It is a Sanskrit word which means a self dwelling place, seat, or residence
In other words, this is where your person/personality resides!
The color is Orange 🍊 the color of optimism & joy
Ruled by Cancer which is cardinal summer, The Sun and the Moon

Activation 6 months to 2.5 years
Development 7-14years of age in the Hindu system
Placement is on the 9th sphere of the Tree of Life
Best gem for it is the Bloodstone gem 💎 blood cleanser removes negative environmental energy, realign with the heart ❤️ Blood flow is heavily involved with the sex act and creative activities. Clean blood is necessary for the sacral to function properly and is super important to our bodies overall.

The Sacral is connected to the Sacrum which is sacred or holy
This area is the Holy place of the body while the mind above is the holy of holies our subconscious
Emotions derive from what's in our subconscious programming
Emotions are fluid like water, like the ocean... like water in a glass, emotions need to be given boundaries or poured into a vessel to get proper use
Efficiency is key here
The Sacral is More than sex

WHY IS THE SACRAL IMPORTANT?

Too many stop at the association with sex not understanding that sex is just simply the creative life force.

It's where your personality is developed.
Personality is made of thoughts feelings and behaviors
The sacral is the house of the Ego states of the child, adult, and parent and develops between ages 1-3
Some say it is developed between the ages of 6 months to 2.5 years
Hindu says 7-14 years old
6 months sitting up alone, can turn in any direction, able to coordinate food to swallow walk talk
7-14 adolescent years trying to find your way again the awkward years which is also known as the Venus years in Cardology.

Ego controls who you believe you are and who the world tells you you are
Ego is how you show up in the world and deal with others and your environment

Sex alone does not lead to intimacy, connection does, and you can connect without having physical sex... into me see... CONNECTION between people (creativity) DISCONNECT between people (no ability to create).

Connected to the Sacrum bone which means sacred or holy
Holy place while above is the holy of holies our subconscious
Emotions derive from what's in our subconscious programming

Blending of emotions... what is their emotional state? What is your emotional state? You emotional state resides in your ego, living in the sacral, your seat of power. What are you creating or not creating together?

Sex without the root chakra established
Emotional intelligence is needed
Fear guilt shame result from connecting sexually while disconnected
Fear from basic needs not met root/foundation
Guilt from partaking in something you can't afford to truly care for or handle
Shame from inability to rise above circumstances Solar plexus/confidence
Vicious cycle can't get to social intelligence let alone self actualization
(See Chart of Maslow's Hierarchy of Needs, p.19)

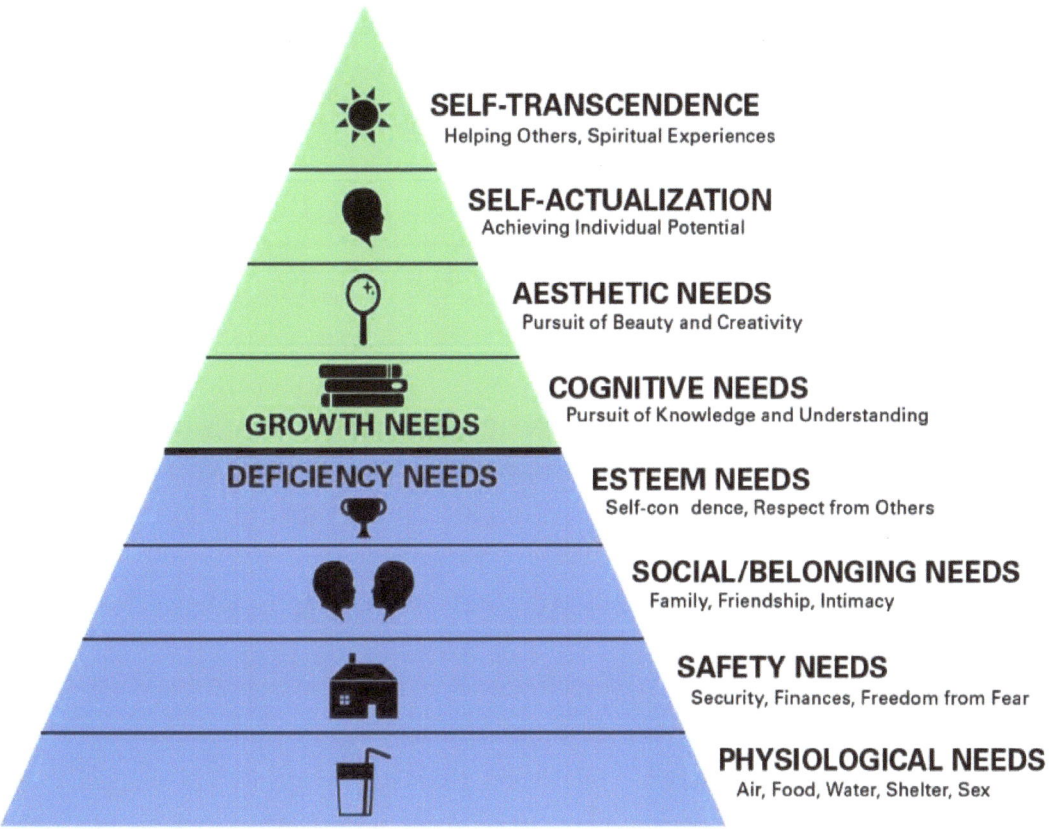

Maslow's Hierarchy of Needs (Internet Source)

See, everyone loves to talk about the root chakra which grounds you to the human experience but the sacral is part of that root system and this is why poor people still indulge in sex while struggling in poverty. Sex in my opinion is a very HUMAN experience. In the ethers we don't need sex as we can create with just a thought. We can also create with our thoughts here on Earth and realize that creation can be positive or negative. As a matter of fact everything you see in this physical realm started with a thought! It came into being by acting on the thought!

The above diagram came from an online Google search about Maslow's Hierarchy of needs. Sex is just as important as air, food, water, and shelter. Although I know the spiritual community at large likes to rank sex as some highly spiritual experience, it is not. Sex is one of our most BASIC needs and is far removed from the self actualization and growth needs of the chart above. Once people's deficiency needs are met, they can then move on to actually "wake up" or become woke. There is something I learned in college called bandwidth. When people's mind is preoccupied with getting basic needs met, they don't have the "bandwidth"to truly self actualize to hear all that spiritual talk and especially not shadow work, lol.

Let me also say this, If you are truly a highly spiritual person, your basic needs will be met so that you can truly focus on spiritual growth. Spiritual people know how to do mundane things. What I am trying to say is if you do not have a profitable business and you are not inhibited in body and mind, you should have a corporate job. It makes me laugh to see a broke spiritual person. A well-developed spiritual person knows how to call upon the Universe and at the same time set an alarm clock to get up and go get the money to pay the bills until better times come along. So don't be foolish and listen to people telling you to quit your job that is taking care of you and helping you build your dreams. Remember, misery loves company.

HOW TO GOVERN THE SACRAL

Learn how to control your waters!
Your waters are your emotional impulses and desires. This is why it's the color orange ruled by Cancer which governs summer which is the Sun and the Moon. This is your ego, your personality, and your mental conditioning from your upbringing when you were very young. You MUST reprogram your mind with higher levels of thinking because thoughts lead to emotions and emotions lead to actions like acting on the emotion of wanting sex!

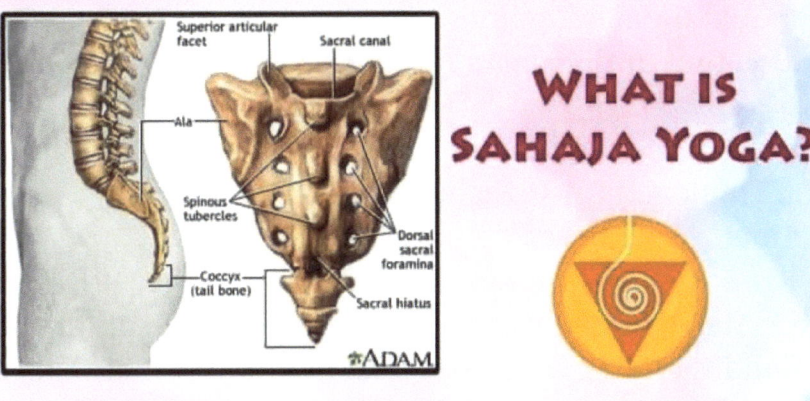

Retain your God seed (Claustrum down to the sacrum to rise back up later) The diagram above came from another Google search about the sacrum or holy bone which houses the sacrum. Notice it is shaped like a triangle. When I was at a museum in Denver, I learned that the triangle is the strongest and most supportive shape of all shapes. Your sacral/sacrum area supports you and keeps you strong so treat it well and with respect.

Every time your birth sign is in the moon you will receive heightened intuition and be flooded with creative ideas when not having sex during this time. Sex depletes your waters and your creativity. The moon is in a sign from 2 to 3 days... this is 10% of the month. This is the true essence of tithing when you allow your seed seating in your holy bone/sacral region germinate and return to the Most High which is your Holy of Holies, your Mind!

This monthly practice of abstinence teaches self control for higher spiritual purposes. Napoleon Hill in his book Think and grow Rich calls this practice sex transmutation and it is also something you can see athletes adhering to it before big games or championships. I even remember in high school the guys would be talking about how they can't be with their girl until after the game because Coach told them not to indulge in sex until after the game. I never truly understood that until I began my spiritual journey in 2003.

Here are some resources and reading on Sex transmutation
Napoleon Hill, Think and Grow Rich, Chapter 11
Ra Un Nefer Amen, Metu Neter Volume 1, pgs. 346-350

Speaking of the Metu Neter, I had an epiphany when I read the above pages on the Kemetic Goddess Auset which governs Ego, and I wrote the following winning formula:

WINNING FORMULA FOR BALANCED SACRAL ENERGY

Pair sacral/sexual energy/life force with
Amen which is Detachment
Ausar which is Knowledge of the self
Tehuti which is Wisdom ie good counsel advice intuition
Seker which is structure planning organization
Maat which is Divine law and reciprocity
Herukhuti which is Justice which is the enforcement of laws/boundaries and enforcing the law & creating boundaries on oneself requires courage
Heru, which is your Will, your self determination which builds character
Het Heru which is Beauty and a joyful attitude
Sebek which is Education and Scholarship (we do need it)
Auset which is the sacral where the ego resides which is used for Imagination

Blending those Kemetic attributes with sexual and creative energy will bring balance to your entire life as you truly begin to control your waters. Remember that we are mostly water, and it behooves us to gain victory in this area if we will ascend to higher heights.

Pearl of Wisdom & Power Moment

Photo Courtesy of Pexels.com by **Елизавета Крючкина**

"SOME THINGS ARE SACRED"

In this modern world, nothings seems sacred anymore, especially sex or anything with a sexual tone. It is important to treat this basic human need as sacred because as a triangle it is the very thing that can either uphold life or crumble life if left broken and unbalanced.

WALKING IN YOUR DESIGN FOR 1 HOUR AND 25 MINUTES

In order to understand who you are, you must first understand what you are made out of! Although I am not religious, I use the Christian scriptures and break them down using esoteric and occult knowledge. Let's take a look at some key verses here to truly discover and who and what God is.

Gen 2:7

And the LORD God formed man *of* the dust of the ground and breathed into his nostrils the breath of life; and man became a living soul.

Who is the Lord?
Yehova הָוָא **hâvâ',** haw-vaw'; or הָוָה hâvâh; a primitive root supposed to mean properly, TO BREATHE; to be (in the sense of existence):—be, × have. אָוָה **'âvâh,** aw-vaw'; a primitive root; to wish for:—covet, (greatly) desire, be desirous, long, lust (after). ה **hâyâh,** haw-yaw; a primitive root to exist, i.e. be or become, come to pass (always emphatic, and not a mere copula or auxiliary):—beacon, × altogether, be(-come), accomplished, committed, like), break, cause, come (to pass), do, faint, fall, follow, happen, × have, last, pertain, quit (one-) self, require, × use.

Who is God?
Elohim! Multiple gods!
Eloah means god, god-like one, mighty one
  1. mighty men, men of rank, mighty heroes
  2. angels
  3. god, false god, (demons, IMAGINATIONS) DISPOSITIONS
  4. God, the one true God, Jehovah
 2. mighty things in nature
 3. strength, power
A Ram (Aries) known for taking aggressive swift action
אַיִל **'ayil,** ah'-yield properly, strength; hence, anything strong; specifically a chief (politically); also a ram (from his strength); a pilaster (as a strong support); an oak or other strong tree:—mighty (man), lintel, oak, post, ram, tree. 1   prominence, body, belly (contemptuous)! nobles, wealthy men

אֱלִיל **ʼûwl,** ool; from an unused root meaning to twist, i.e. (by implication) be strong; the body (as being rolled together); also powerful:—mighty, strength. Elohim is plural

1. rulers, judges
2. divine ones
3. angels
4. gods

2. (plural intensive - singular meaning)
   1. god, goddess
   2. godlike one
   3. works or special possessions of God
   4. the (true) God
   5. God

Eloah means "the body powerfully rolled together"! Isn't your body put together in a powerful way? If Eloah, God, breathed into us, then what does that make us? God!

Roman 8:1
There is therefore now no condemnation to them which are in Christ Jesus, who walk not after the flesh, but after the Spirit.

Who is Christ Jesus?
Christ means to rub with oil through contact. **Root Word (Etymology)**
From a form of an obsolete prim chao (to "gape" or "yawn") taking in BREATH!
Consecrate, late Middle English: from Latin *consecrat-* 'dedicated, devoted as sacred,' from the verb *consecrare*, from *con-* (expressing intensive force) + *sacrare* 'dedicate,' from *sacer* 'sacred.' connected with God (or the gods). late Middle English: past participle of archaic *sacre* 'consecrate,' from Old French *sacrer*, from Latin *sacrare*, from *sacer*, *sacr-* 'holy.' Holy is Old English *hālig*, of Germanic origin; related to Dutch and German *heilig*, also to whole. Whole is Old English *hāl*, of Germanic origin; related to Dutch *heel* and German *heil*, also to hail2. The spelling with *wh-* (reflecting a dialect pronunciation with *w-*) first appeared in the 15th century. Hail is a shout or call used to attract attention. Whole is a thing that is complete in itself.

Holy means healthy. Spirit means Breath. You are whole. Complete in yourself. You don't NEED anything else! And there is NO CONDEMNATION when you are being you! You are connected to Source, and you ARE that source! How? The BREATH!

Jesus is a verb not a person! Something you do! An Action!

.Jesus in the Heb yaw-shah, to be liberated, be saved, be delivered,**yâsha'** יָשַׁע
1. to be saved (in battle), be victorious
2. (Hiphil)to save, deliver, to save from moral troubles, to give victory

To be delivered but how? Through the breath! Something I discovered in my yoga practice is that deep nostril breathing and being aware of your breath brings your entire being back to peace and balance. This equilibrium helps you to focus and easily gain clarity to find solutions to your problems.

Let us find out what the breath is through a few key words & definitions:

Spirit
means to breathe, to blow, of the wind Hebrew root is ψύχω **psýchō,** psoo'-kho; a primary verb; TO BREATHE (voluntarily but gently, thus differing on the one hand which denotes properly a forcible respiration; and which refers properly to an inanimate breeze), i.e. (by implication, of reduction of temperature by evaporation) to chill (figuratively):—wax cold.

Soul
Hebrew נָפַשׁ **nâphash,** naw-fash'; a primitive root; TO BREATHE; passively, to be breathed upon, i.e. (figuratively) refreshed (as if by a current of air):—(be) refresh selves (-ed).

PSYCHE
mid 17th century: via Latin from Greek *psukhē* 'BREATH, life, soul'.

So it seems like Spirit, Soul, and Psyche which is your mind all mean Breath or to breathe! I want you to notice that the BODY is not included here! This means that the body is just the house for the spirit, soul, and psyche which is your breath! You are made of God which is Breath! This is your true essence! Remember there is no condemnation when you just being and breathing!

Condemnation: Greek **krínō,** kree'-no ,call in question, sentence to think.
   1   to pronounce an opinion concerning right and wrong, to be

judged, i.e. summoned to trial that one's case may be examined, and judgment passed upon it, to pronounce judgment, to subject to censure, of those who act the part of judges or arbiters in matters of common life, or pass judgment on the deeds and words of others, to rule, govern

Now let's look at another biblical text and see if we can determine the difference between copying someone and authenticity:

Proverbs 16:9
A man's heart devises his way, But the LORD directs his steps.

Devised or directed?

Devise
חָשַׁב **châshab,** khaw-shab'; a primitive root; properly, to plait or interpenetrate, i.e. (literally) to weave or (generally) to fabricate; figuratively, to plot or contrive (usually in a malicious sense); hence (from the mental effort) to think, regard, value, compute:—(make) account (of), conceive, consider, count, cunning (man, work, workman), devise, esteem, find out, forecast, hold, imagine, impute, invent, be like, mean, purpose, reckon(-ing be made), regard, think.

Direct
כּוּן **kûwn,** koon; a primitive root; properly, to be erect (i.e. stand perpendicular); hence (causatively) to set up, in a great variety of applications, whether literal (establish, fix, prepare, apply), or figurative (appoint, render sure, proper or prosperous):—certain(-ty), confirm, direct, faithfulness, fashion, fasten, firm, be fitted, be fixed, frame, be meet, ordain, order, perfect, (make) preparation, prepare (self), provide, make provision, (be, make) ready, right, set (aright, fast, forth), be stable, (e-) stablish, stand, tarry, × very deed.

Contrived or appointed?

Contrive
create or bring about (an object or a situation) by deliberate use of skill and artifice. manage to do something foolish or create an undesirable situation. Middle English: from Old French *contreuve-*, stressed stem of *controver* 'imagine, invent,' from medieval Latin *contropare* 'compare.'

Appoint
assign a job or role to (someone). determine or decide on (a time or a place. late Middle English: from Old French *apointer*, from *a point* 'to a point.'

What does it mean to appoint people?

Appoint
to name or assign to a position, an office, or the like; designate: to appoint a new **treasurer**; to appoint a judge to the bench. to determine by authority or agreement; fix; set: to appoint a time for the meeting. Law. to designate (a person) to take the benefit of an estate created by a deed or will.

What does it mean when you are contriving?

Contrivance; plural noun: **contrivances**
the use of skill to bring something about or create something. A contrivance is **a gadget or device that can be used for some particular purpose**. The spinning blade of a blender is a contrivance that turns fruits and yogurt into a tasty smoothie. Yum. A contrivance is a useful device or tool.

What about a tool for Strategy?

Stratagem is a tactic or artifice designed to gain the upper hand, especially one involving underhanded dealings or deception while trick is something designed to fool or swindle.

Why did you look up all those definitions Michelle? Because I am trying to show you the difference between when you are authentically being you and when you are trying too hard to be something you are not!
So how are you using your imagination? To concoct some scheme to get ahead or are you just being who you already are? Are you Just simply BREATHING?

Are YOU trying to make something happen or are you allowing life's experiences to inspire you? Allowing your spirit, soul, and psyche to Breathe into you?

Now let's look at the word imagination and some Hebrew words related to it

Imagination
the faculty or action of forming new ideas, or images or concepts of external objects not present to the senses. Middle English: via Old French from Latin *imaginatio(n-*), from the verb *imaginari* 'picture to oneself,' from *imago, imagin-* 'image.'

Devise
חָשַׁב **châshab,** khaw-shab'; a primitive root; properly, to plait or interpenetrate, i.e. (literally) to weave or (generally) to fabricate; figuratively, to plot or contrive (usually in a malicious sense); hence (from the mental effort) to think, regard, value, compute:—(make) account (of), conceive, consider, count, cunning (man, work, workman), devise, esteem, find out, forecast, hold, **IMAGINE**, impute, invent, be like, mean, purpose, reckon(-ing be made), regard, think.

Plotting (Cunning inventions ie scheme, a form of thinking)
מַחֲשָׁבָה **machăshâbâh,** makh-ash-aw-baw'; or מַחֲשֶׁבֶת machăshebeth; contrivance, i.e. (concretely) a texture, machine, or (abstractly) intention, plan (whether BAD, a plot; or GOOD, advice):—cunning (work), curious work, device(-sed), **IMAGINATION**, invented, means, purpose, thought.

This is wrong use of imagination... you are a mad scientist making a mess from not following your appointed design... you are creating something without understanding HOW and WHY the thing was made. When you are not following your instructions, you will wind up creating a monster! You simply don't know what you are made of because you wont look into it! You are contriving by using "technology and machinery" when you are not focusing on your breath... the essence of who you are. That is what you are doing when you are copying or imitating someone. You are fabricating because their story is not your story. You have a fantasy prone personality!

Fantasy prone personality (FPP) is **a disposition or personality trait in which a person experiences a lifelong extensive and deep involvement in fantasy.** This disposition is an attempt, at least in part, to better describe "overactive imagination" or "living in a dream world".

Are you living in a dream world wishing you were someone else or had their talents, gifts, or calling? Why are you dishonoring the God that you are? Why are you disregarding your very breath which is your life???

Imagination is so vast that there is no need to copy anyone else. Let's take a look at seven distinct kinds of imagination and the ways you can use them from an article I found online during my research.

https://writingcooperative.com/understanding-your-creative-engine-the-8-types-of-imagination-5265ebdae79f

Effectuative imagination USING EXISTING INFO

Intellectual Imagination DOING RESEARCH FOR INFO

Imaginative Fantasy BEING INSPIRED BREATHED INTO

Empathy DETACHING FROM SELF EXPERIENCE

Strategic Imagination WORKING WITH STRENGTHS WEAKNESSES

Emotional Imagination EMOTIONAL INTELLIGENCE AND AWARENESS

Dreams UNCONSCIOUS WORK

Those examples of imagination are all ways that can help you without pretending to be something or someone you are not.
Walking in your design means studying you. Becoming a lifelong student of you! Getting to know what makes you, you and to finally think for yourself.

Once you discover who you are it's just the beginning. Work within your parameters. You are going to discover some negative traits and weaknesses. Saying "This is me" is not good enough. Strategize how to overcome your weak points.

Here are a few tools to discover who you are... There are SO MANY more than these listed here!

Your birth chart- Time passages app or Astro.com
Human Design
Gene keys
Ray Dalio's Principles
Disc assessment
Carl Jung personality tests
Ancestry/Genealogy
Myers Briggs personality
Gallup Clifton Strengths
Fascination
Cardology
Astrology
Numerology
Personality tests
Archetype tests
Asking your elders about your family because you needed what they had to become who you are
Asking people in your life about you (I sought coworkers, boss, family, friends feedback) But do not do this until you have firm sense of you are within because some people can project their programming unto you and if you do not know who you are, you will take on something that is not yours!

You will begin to see your design that was breathed into you as you go on a journey of self discovery.

WINNING FORMULA FOR WALKING IN YOUR DESIGN

Your gifts are not for you, They are for serving the collective
You are not for everybody; Your tribe is waiting on you
Finding out who you are should be your life's work
Seek feedback once you have done your own self discovery
Do not compare as you are meant to be unique & walk your path

Pearl of Wisdom & Power Moment

Photo courtesy of Pexels.com by XO Motion

"SUNDAY SERVICE"

Your true hour of worship should be finding out what you were put here to do. What is the point of entering a building with fancy clothes when you have not even step foot into your own heart to discover who you are and who you are here to serve in the collective?

April 26, 2022

Whatever you add to I AM, you become! For 1 hour 32 minutes

The first thing to understand first is that I AM works Positive or Negative!

History and Etymology for I
Pronoun Middle English, from Old English ic; Latin ego, Greek egō

What is the Letter I?
The 9th letter of the English alphabet
A grade meaning incomplete
An imaginary unit or symbol
the one who is speaking or writing
someone aware of possessing a personal individuality

In numerology, the number 9 is represented by the I and has empath energy.

An Empath one who experiences the emotions of others & emotions come from thought, the mind
Telepathy communication is from one mind to another
A Telephone is an instrument reproducing sounds at a distance

The difference between empathy and sympathy

Empathy
the action of understanding, being aware of, being sensitive to, and vicariously experiencing the feelings, thoughts, and experience of another of either the past or present without having the feelings, thoughts, and experience fully communicated in an objectively <u>explicit</u> manner

Sympathy (which comes from the Greek sym, meaning "together," and pathos, referring to feelings or emotion) is used when one person shares the feelings of another; an example is when one experiences sadness when someone close is experiencing grief or loss.

Empathy is also related to Em, which is from the Greek meaning within, inside. Empathy differs from sympathy because it is carrying an implication of greater emotional distance. With empathy, you can imagine or understand how someone might feel, without necessarily having those feelings yourself.

Soooo, empaths are not helpless! In empathy, you do have control and you don't have to take on the emotions of others! You UNDERSTAND without FEELING... That is the definition of empathy. Distance is involved!

SYMPathy is when you involve yourself in FEELING what someone else is feeling. You are not an empath but a symp/simp when you take on the feelings of others.

When it comes to you, the I, the ego, the empath, distance is involved! You are not like anyone else! You are unique and your situation is unique!

The I by itself is incomplete! It needs the word AM which is a form of the word be. Another way to say AM is the word BE. Let's take a look at what it means.

Present tense first-person singular of <u>BE</u>
a broadcasting system, a radio receiver
Be means to receive, to exist, be present, occur or take place

Etymology of BE
Old English *beon*, *beom*, *bion* "be, exist, come to be, become, happen," from Proto-Germanic *bíju-* "I am, I will be." This "b-root" is from PIE root **<u>*bheue-</u>** "to be, exist, grow

So the AM works by receiving which makes it an empath! The Ego works with the empathetic telepathic messages from the cosmos. You are literally bringing heaven down to earth.

Exodus 3:13-14

And Moses said unto God, Behold, **when** I come unto the children of Israel, and shall say unto them, The God of your fathers hath sent me unto you; and they shall say to me, What **is** his name? what shall I say unto them?
And God said unto Moses, **I AM THAT I AM**: and he said, Thus shalt thou say unto the children of Israel, I AM hath sent me unto you.

Hebrew Definition of I AM

הָוָא **hâvâ',** haw-vaw'; or הָוָה hâvâh; a primitive root supposed to mean properly, **to breathe**; to be, to desire, to become, to happen

What are you saying about yourself, what are you **breathing out** when I AM comes **to** you?

What comes after your I AM?

You breathing right? You are I AM **RIGHT NOW!**

Rev Ike, in the video I played in the room that day, said that we are proclaiming to **be** God when we say I am!
You are taking the name of God!
Now that You have taken it, what are you going to do with all of that power?!!!!

What is going to come after your I AM???

WINNING FORMULA FOR USING YOUR I AM

I AM IS A PROCLAMATION. Watch what you are DECLARING.
Use positive present tense statements with I AM
Negative statements work too, just not for your highest good!
Say your I AM's till you KNOW them (intimacy)

Pearl of Wisdom & Power Moment

Photo courtesy of Pexels.com by Cotton Bro Studios

"WHAT ARE YOU WAITING FOR"

You got all dressed up, you showed up, and now… you just sitting there. Waiting. What are you waiting for??? Use your I AM already to bring heaven down to earth and stop waiting for someone to come save you. You have the power to save yourself. Stop waiting for people to show up for you. Show up for yourself. Use the power within.

<u>**May 24, 2022**</u>

<u>**Nine: Key to Manifestation for 2 hours and 14 minutes**</u>

Nikola Tesla is known for his fascination with 369. Let's take a look at some facts about 369.

3 father mother child/the triangle/ harmony wisdom and understanding/ think speak act/ red, yellow, blue makes all colors/ birth life death
6 carbon, protons, electrons, neutrons/Hexagon Venus
9 it is all and at the same time nothing, singularity and the vacuum. The basic rules of magnetism states **Like poles repel each other. Unlike poles attract each other**.

369 is 9 and referred to as Spirit which is 10 which is 9 because you go thru 9 before getting to the 1 and the zero which is the womb of creation!
124578 is the Material world and equals 27 which is 9!

123456789 contains all the numbers, it equals 45... 4 and 5 is 9! I love Math!
Foundation like a chair 🪑 sturdy, loyal like a chair, 4 upholds you foundation of a house but also tears down old constructs to make way for change
5 is about change which is true freedom
Freedom is the ability to change
9 see the Loop in the head... this is mental power which you need to change

Nikola Tesla said:
3 represents our connection to source or the universe, and our creative self-expression (This is Jupiter energy)
6 represents our inner strength and harmony (This is Venus)
9 represents our inner rebirth (as in letting go of what no longer serves us and changing into who we are becoming) This is Mars/Pluto energy.

9 is Aries ♈ and Scorpio ♏ the 1st head and the last, the tail
Aries is all about Springing into Action a Cardinal sign that starts the new year
Scorpio is a fixed water sign that is about personal transformation and creation as it governs the seat of the soul with its ruler as Pluto and ancient ruler as Mars (first and the last) Both signs govern the ego the head Aries and the tail, the Scorpio which is the tailbone, your sacrum or sacral where your

personality resides also where your life force or creativity resides. Jupiter helps you to expand in the womb of creation as it is still considered the ruler of Pisces in the Kemetic tradition. Venus is exalted in Pisces and helps you build your creations. The 9 works with them all!

The number 9 is the soul solution to every achievement number issue in numerology!

nines (n.)

in phrase *to the nines* "to perfection, fully, elaborately" (1787) first attested in Burns, apparently preserves the ancient notion of the perfection of the number as three times three (such as the nine Muses, the *Nine Worthies*, ancient personages famous for bravery, and the nine orders of angels). T]the *Book of St. Albans,* in the sections on blasonry, lays great stress on the *nines* in which all perfect things (orders of angels, virtues, articles of chivalry, differences of coat armour, etc.) occur. [Weekley] No one seems to consider that it might be a corruption and misdivision of *to then anes*, literally "for the one (purpose or occasion)," a similar construction to that which yielded **nonce** (q.v.). Century Dictionary suspects it is a corruption of Middle English *to then eyne* "to the eyes."the cardinal number one more than eight or one less than ten; the number which is one more than eight.

The number 9 is **perfection** of all things that occur. (Perfect ending). complete (symbolizes completion) to the one ☝ to the eye 👁
The 9 is associated with the kundalini (lies in 3 and 1/2 coils or 3 by 3) which begins in a coiled state at the base/root or sacral region (this is the region of ego and creation) Lets take a look at the esoteric meaning of 9 in Christian literature.

Rev 5:1 The book or story within you!
Then I saw in the right hand of him who was seated on the throne a scroll written within and on the back, sealed with seven seals.

This is the chakras and the uncoiled kundalini energy … the nine!

Book of Revelations 11:3
And I will give *power* unto my two witnesses, and they shall prophesy a thousand two hundred *and* threescore days, clothed in sackcloth.

Three score means 6 times 10 or 60
1260 is three- and one-half times. And equals 9.
Witness in Hebrew means martyr or one who is a spectator or **witness** of anything (3rd eye) to record the event.

The 1260 relates to the kundalini coiled up in your sacral region before activation and the two witnesses are the pineal and the pituitary that work with and bring alive the kundalini or life force energy! They record the event! I could say more but that would take another book!

Pingala means Pineal
Pineal is masculine Sun 🌞 Personality outer Electricity seat of Soul initiate related to heaven
The main function of the pineal gland is to **receive information about the state of the light-dark cycle from the environment and convey this information to produce and secrete the hormone melatonin**. It rules Night, sleep wake heart rhythms circadian

Ida means Pituitary
Pituitary gland is feminine Moon 🙂 emotions inner Magnetic receives and related to earth
Helps to control growth, blood pressure, energy management, all functions of the sex organs, thyroid glands and metabolism as well as some aspects of pregnancy, childbirth, breastfeeding, water/salt concentration In the kidneys, temperature regulation and pain relief

For anything to come into being to be created, The higher and the lower must marry! The two must marry! They must consummate! No consummation means nothing can be created and brought forth into this realm! This is why there is an attack on the basic structure of relationship to bring confusion so that NOTHING manifests.

The number nine is about duality!
Nine is the problem and contains all of the problems but is also the solution to all of the numbers!
It's nothing and everything at the same time!
The number 9 is the soul solution to every achievement number issue in numerology!

You can't just daydream with the 9. The 9 is humanitarian. That's responsibility. You must do the work.
Find out who you are, get strong in it, then let it go
Don't just dream! Take actions!
Affirmations don't work unless you do!

The I Ching states everything in the universe is seeking harmony and goes thru cycles of imbalance and disharmony to balance and harmony again.
So you must go thru endings (the nine) to get to a beginning!
Stop being afraid of starting and ending something!
Everything begins with springing into action!
But Then it must come to an end before starting all over again!
The 9 is the gateway between beginning and ending
You meet the 9 coming and going!
The 9 is in the I Ching as Heaven Initiation Masculine
The 9 is in the I Ching as Earth Receptive Feminine
This maintains balance and harmony which opens the door for manifestation
You must be flexible and be willing to change and receive from Source
Your transformation and creativity must be both moving/flowing but also permanent.
Manifestation is about duality
It is all and nothing at the same time!
It is action and reception at the same time
It is ebb and flow and stop and go!
You being material (3 and 6) MUST work with SPIRIT(9) for ANYTHING to manifest!

WINNING FORMULA FOR MANIFESTATION

You need your ego to manifest!

Everything starts with an ending before you can begin

You must marry your masculine & feminine energies to create in this realm

You must cooperate with Heaven which is Spirit and be open to receive on Earth

Pearl of Wisdom & Power Moment

Photo courtesy of Pexels.com by Mervi Rep

"MARRY YOUR MASCULINE & YOUR FEMININE"

Men can wear pearls and jewels and women can wear pants and play sports! Who ever said one could not do what the other does? While there are biological differences and limitations in some respects, both should coexist in the same space to truly manifest anything in this material world. You must embody both in the proper place and time for true success.

June 21, 2022

Shine Bright! Summer Solstice for 4 hours and 4 minutes

I did not realize that I joined clubhouse app as a member on during the summer solstice on the first day of Cancer Season in 2021. And then, I later chose a pearl, something that comes out of the ocean which is ruled over by the Moon which rules Cancer Season along with the Sun… You can't make this stuff up! Enjoy the lesson I gave the day of my one-year Clubhouse anniversary.

Integrity is integration of your words with your behavior! Do the words that come out of your mouth align with the actions you take? Can people trust you? Are you a person of excellence? Are you worried about who is going to see it? The painter of the Sistine Chapel was Michelangelo. When I was in Italy staring at it at the Vatican, I learned that he spent time painting in a corner no one would probably look at. People wondered why he would spend time painting a corner. He told them people may not see it, but God will see it. WOW!!!! Michelangelo was not doing this for people to see it, he was only concerned that Source will see it! Do you realize that everything successful is done with mathematical precision! There is a cycle and a season to everything in the universe… an excellent person is never satisfied! They keep going and growing! If you are not growing you are already dying! This is how you take advantage of the SunShine in the Summer Solstice!

Let us look at the energy of the day
Cancer season June 21
Today is the first day of summer! This year it is The day of the six!
6/3/6= 15= 6

Today is also a 9 clubs day in Cardology.
Completion high universal vibration and it demands individual self discipline patience and perseverance. A positive attitude is a must! Ruled by Saturn and Venus… a labor of love! Sacrifice, diligence, flexible, creativity, this is the entrepreneurial spirit! In the spiritual spread it is the 6 of diamonds, karmic what do you value and how are you handling your money… 9 signifies the end and sets the stage for your beginning, so what is your mindset?

Two cycles of man
Cycle 1 is 144 years divided into 7-year cycles = 20.57 = 14= 5 change
Cycle 2 is 365 days into 7 (52) days birthday to birthday

If the earth were not tilted and spins we would not have seasons
23.5 which is 10 and goes thru 20th thru the 23rd

Summer solstice arrived at 5:14 Est = 10 which is source code
This is the Ace cards of the deck which are the natural born leaders
It's time to step up and be a leader, a pioneer! Standout as an individual! Some people will get their feelings hurt in this season, but you have to stand on your own two feet. You must transcend your ego and get into your spiritual bag to do the impossible! You need patience, tolerance, compassion and to take responsibility for your own actions and not play the blame game!

Sun is at its highest northern point ...
Pauses to go in reverse for the next 6 months to where? The Winter solstice! This means the focus should be outward! Time to get to work get strong for harvest and prepare for a season of rest and stillness in winter ❄

John 9:4
I must work the works of him that sent me, while it is day: the night cometh, when no man can work.

Let me break down the words work

1 Work: to make gains, to acquire, to get it done, an undertaking
2 Works: your employment, your occupation, occupied with
3 Work: cannot make gains! There is a time, a cycle when you cannot make gains

Let me break down the entire verse
I (the word)
is condensed version of me... no mistake this is about you! Involves no one else! It is an accusative pronoun, The objective (or accusative) case pronouns are **me, you (singular), him/her/it, us, you (plural), them and whom**. (Notice that form of you and it does not change.) The objective case is used

when something is being done to (or given to, etc.) the finger is pointing back to you...

Him
late 16th century: from French *idiome*, or via late Latin from Greek *idiōma* 'private property, peculiar phraseology', from *idiousthai* 'make one's own', from *idios* 'own, private'.

This is an idiom which means that it is a personal private meaning... this is not about gender. It is about energy at work in your life. It names any and everything you are subject to, Source the energy in charge of the Universe and your life. Raining cats and dogs saying. What is your private understanding and relationship to the energies in charge the boss of your life? Do you know your boss?

Day
metaph., "the day" is regarded as the time for abstaining from indulgence, vice, crime, because acts of the sort are perpetrated at night and in darkness. of the last day of this present age! A sense of responsibility and urgency!

Night
metaph. the time when work ceases, from a root meaning 'to disappear' the time of death! the time for deeds of sin and shame! the time of moral stupidity and darkness, the time when the weary and also the drunken give themselves up to slumber

Man
it literally means nobody, absolutely positively no! again not about gender, God forbid that you should even think you could do some work... it's a no for me dog!

What is the summer solstice saying to us?
Do your work while it's day!
Longest day of the season! You can get A LOT DONE!
Tuesday is Mars day, Aries is exalted in the sun
Aries rules the 1st house so you can't go to work if you have not put yourself first, when the sun comes out Aries says let's get it cracking
Leo ruled by the sun is exalted in Neptune Leo is 5th house (spirituality, womb of creation 12th house, the pronoun I, this is about getting YOUR work

done, not someone else, not being occupied with what someone else is doing! It's showtime! Time to get on stage and perform Time for you to shine bright!)

Shine

Old English *scinan* "shed light, be radiant, be resplendent, illuminate," of persons, "be conspicuous" (class I strong verb; past tense *scan*, past participle *scinen*), from Proto-Germanic **skeinanan* (source also of Old Saxon and Old High German *skinan*, Old Norse and Old Frisian *skina*, Dutch *schijnen*, German *scheinen*, Gothic *skeinan* "to shine, appear"), which perhaps is from a PIE root **skai-* "to shine, to gleam" (source also of Old Church Slavonic *sinati* "to flash up, shine"). Transitive meaning "to black (boots)" is from 1610s. Related: *Shined* (in the shoe polish sense), otherwise *shone*; *shining*.

In the military I shined my shoes by put black polish on my boots and I would buff it until it appeared shiny on the toe! You may have to put some black on you and buff it out to get a shine!

Apply leather conditioner to your boots once a week. Otherwise it will start to crack! You must condition yourself often because it wears off!

Bright

Sanskrit *bhrajate* "shines, glitters;" Lithuanian *brėkšti* "to dawn;" Welsh *berth* "bright, beautiful."
"radiating or reflecting light," Old English *bryht*, metathesis of *beorht* "bright; splendid; clear-sounding; beautiful; divine," from Proto-Germanic **berhtaz* "bright" (source also of Old Saxon *berht*, Old Norse *bjartr*, Old High German *beraht*, Gothic *bairhts* "bright"), from PIE root ***bhereg-** "to shine; bright, white." Meaning "quick-witted, having brilliant mental qualities" is from 1741.

Gemini ♊ the 3rd sign is quick witted! On the cusp of Cancer who is sensitive!
Ruled by the 5 and Mercury which is change, freedom moves quickly, it does not dilly dally around!
Cancer the 4th sign , foundation, loyalty, trust, this is about home! The work you do will be your home in winter! What kind of foundation are you building while it's day? Cause do not think you can work when night comes!

WINNING FORMULA FOR SHINING BRIGHT IN THE SUN

Know your employer and your employment! Do you know the energies at play in your life? Do you know what those energies true purpose is and the type of work it wants out of you? Do you know the work you are put here to do?

Learn to say no to some of your feelings and impulses. In school, nice outside but doing my homework. Wow she did it... feelings of inadequacy when you see someone did it while you didn't! Just say no you got work to do! Winter is coming man! No to external influences too!

Practice compassion for self and others this is Cancer ♋ you will make mistakes. It won't go as planned. Perfection does not exist. Lol my book process lol

Keep a positive mental attitude! Your brain does not know the difference between real and imagining so why not use it to your advantage, imagine good outcomes! Also watch your diet, not just food!

Change is inevitable during your process! Anticipate change and prepare for it. This means you need to stop and evaluate what you are doing from time to time, in other words learn when to come up for air!

PEARLS OF WISDOM AND POWER MOMENT

Photo courtesy of Pexels.com by Sakthi T

"STRUTT YOUR STUFF"

There is nothing wrong with knowing who you are and what you bring to the table. So strut your stuff. Don't be afraid to show your strength and carry your weaknesses. You went through what you went through for a reason. Everything you experienced in this life experience has brought you here. So why are you not doing the work you were put here to do? Why are you hiding how great you are?

<u>**July 19, 2022**</u>

<u>**The Laws of Wisdom**</u>

When it comes to wisdom, here are my personal takeaways from the videos I just played concerning wisdom:

Video 1:
Are you acting aggressively when opportunity presents itself? That's a wrong move!

Video 2
Free will is acting within boundary conditions. You cannot break the law without consequence. The effect does not happen immediately! You can only change the future by your present behavior

Video 3:
Only those with wisdom and inner strength can act with kindness. You can only act this way when you realize the only person you can change is you! Holding on to anger is like drinking poison expecting the other person to die! Whew! Vices to escape pain are always around you but keeping your mind unclouded is where wisdom comes from

Video 4:
Blend inaction with action. The yin and the yang. The Tao te Ching says Flow like water my friend. Water becomes whatever you put it in! Adapts to its environment like a snake does! Running water never grows stale! Think about how a snake moves! Do we act honestly or are we putting on a show? Snakes blend in with their environment! Water

Let's look at a Bible verse that shows how wise people behave.

Luke 16:8
The rich man had to admire the dishonest rascal for being so **shrewd**. And it is true that the children of this world are more shrewd in dealing with the world around them than are the children of the light.

What is the definition of wise?

Wise

Old English *wis* "learned, sagacious, cunning; sane; prudent, discreet; experienced; having the power of discerning and judging rightly," from Proto-Germanic *wissaz* (source also of Old Saxon, Old Frisian *wis*, Old Norse *viss*, Dutch *wijs*, German *weise* "wise"), from past-participle adjective *wittos* of PIE root **weid-** "to see" (hence "to know"). Modern slang meaning "aware, cunning" first attested 1896. Related to the source of Old English *witan* "to know, wit."

Shrewd

marked by clever discerning awareness and hardheaded acumen. given to <u>wily</u> and artful ways or dealing.

Acumen is the ability to make good judgments and quick decisions, typically in a particular domain. late 16th century: from Latin, 'sharpness, point', from *acuere* 'sharpen' (see acute).

Wily

skilled at gaining an advantage, especially deceitfully.

Wisdom is cunning! Like a serpent!

Discern is perceive or recognize (something). distinguish (someone or something) with difficulty by sight or with the other senses. late Middle English: via Old French from Latin *discernere*, from *dis-* 'apart' + *cernere* 'to separate'

Shrew a small animal but etymology is Perhaps from Proto-Germanic *skraw-*, from PIE *skreu-* "to cut; cutting tool" (see **shred** (n.)), in reference to the shrew's pointed snout. Alternative Old English word for it was *scirfemus*, from *sceorfan* "to gnaw."

King Solomon had to be slick with it! He had to be crafty! He was shrewd! He literally "cut" to the chase it's a dispute between two women. When 2 women were arguing over a baby, he told them to cut the baby in two and the woman who had a bond with the baby was willing to give the baby to the other woman! The real mother cried out. Solomon had to **"con"** to get to the truth! This is wisdom folks! It's cunning!

Here are some other notes I took on readings about wisdom that I found in other spiritual literature:

Bhagavad Gita pg. 35 wisdom does not consider its exclusive role or interests
Sage is one who has authority and is learned...
Free from attachment to results/rewards/consequences Wisdom does nothing yet does everything. One must give up lower "impulses"

A person reacts when they don't have power!
When you think that what somebody chooses to do affects you in some way, you will be triggered every time!

Bhavagad Gita: The sacrifice of wisdom and The flame of wisdom

Pg37 You must control your senses, your reactions, the breath controls them

Tao te Ching pg. 37
You have to get out of your feelings to have true success!
You can't let what other people do get to you
But at the same time know your boundaries, honor yourself by honoring them

Pg 45
The power of yielding and giving up the need to be defensive.
Bruce Lee said at one time, "Be water, my friend"

Pg 99
Yield to other perspectives!

Pg. 67
Know thyself!

Bhagahvad Gita pg. 35 Action and Inaction
Karmic debt from actions or inactions when you do something with intent, ie you know what you are doing... in awareness of taking action and even not taking action, you have activated the law of Justice ... now you are in debt and MUST pay!

Jay Z said it best! Nobody wins when the family feuds! It's not wisdom! The constant back and forth is never ending debt! Spiritual debt becomes physical debt! As above so below!

We can't be vengeful or play tit for tat! That creates debt in the spirit realm!

Universal or cosmic law states that every reaction is a reaction. Bob Marley sings it in his song titled Satisfy My Soul

This is why the wise lives in silence for the most part, and only acts when necessary to defend life
Even walking away quietly at times, picking their battles wisely
Remember there is consequence and reward to every action
Your actions come from your thoughts! Sitting in silence is a science, it's training!

WINNING FORMULA FOR WISDOM

Breathe
Scope the environment
Get detached
Yield Be Still
Pick your battles wisely
Know who you are

PEARLS OF WISDOM & POWER MOMENT

Photo courtesy of Pexels.com by Cotton Bro Studios

"WISDOM IS DARKNESS BLENDED WITH THE LIGHT"

You ever heard that saying "Don't hate the player, learn how to play the game"? Well, that's wisdom. You thought it was all love and light, but it has a dark element to it. To truly be wise you must understand human nature and that our natures have a dark side to it. The one who understands how to integrate the dark with the light for the perfect touch of shrewdness can and will rule the word and all the elements in it.

Honoring Yourself and the 4 of diamonds

Let's talk about honoring yourself and the energy of the day, 4 of diamonds and what that means for you.

Video discussion
A dollar is still a dollar. You have never lost your worth no matter what has happened to you!
Who are you following, cooperating with? That can and will influence your values what you honor or give weight to! Why do we give weight to things that are not on a solid foundation! Test everything!
Jordan Peterson you don't create your values, you discover them! It takes time for things to happen or change … you are led by your values.

No two people are exactly alike! Even a marriage couple has different paths!

Once you learned the foundation of something, then it's time to make it your own.

You have to honor value yourself before you can expect anyone else to honor value you!

Value is Honor

The four of diamonds is Saturn Venus in the Spiritual spread boundaries, hard work, and values
Sitting in the 5 hearts challenged by 5 of clubs
It's Neptune Venus in the life spread
Sitting in 5 hearts challenged by 5 of ♠ It's Mercury card is 2 ♠

5 times 4 = 20 which equals 2! The two is your mental programming and thinking which is where your thoughts that come from that give roots to your feelings. How you feel and what you think builds the foundation of your level of cooperation!

Saturn is about hard work and discipline. Neptune is about creativity and creating in secret. Mercury is about gathering intel so you can make some judgments about things and CHOOSE your preferences in Venus... ie your likes and dislikes.

4 is about stability and putting in the work to create solid foundation which may require you to tear down before you can build. But avoid being stubborn!

5 is about change but also curiosity which is openness to variety and adventure. Don't use things to escape the work required!

2 is about cooperation and balance although sometimes you may have to stand alone, avoid getting lost in collabing with others!

Heart is about emotion which come from what you believe to be true or untrue

Clubs is about the way you think which comes from repetitive programs via environment

Spades ♠ are about mastery which is a long journey not a short trip

This means 417 days' worth of hours, or **3 hours a day** for 3,333 days--a little over 9 years

417 is 12/3, 3 hours a day, 3333=12/3 which equals 9 which is 10 the completion of a cycle and beginning of a new one!

What does this have to do with honoring yourself?

Honor is a noun and a verb. A thing and an action.

honor (n.)
c. 1200, *onur*, "glory, renown, fame earned," from Anglo-French *honour*, Old French *onor*, *honor* "honor, dignity, distinction, position; victory, triumph" (Modern French *honneur*), from Latin *honorem* (nominative *honos*, the form used by Cicero, but later *honor*) "honor, dignity, office, reputation," which is of unknown origin. In Middle English, it also could mean "splendor, beauty; excellence." Until 17c., *honour* and *honor* were equally frequent; the former now preferred in England, the latter in U.S. by influence of Noah Webster. Meaning "feminine purity, a woman's chastity" first attested late 14c. ***Honor roll*** in the scholastic sense attested by 1872.

honor (v.)
mid-13c., *honuren*, "to do honor to, show respect to," from Old French *onorer*, *honorer* "respect, esteem, revere; welcome; present" (someone with something), from Latin *honorare* "to honor," from *honor* "honor, dignity, office, reputation" (see **honor** (n.)). From c. 1300 as "confer honors on." From c.

1300 as "to respect, follow" (teachings, etc.). In the commercial sense of "accept a bill due, etc.," it is recorded from 1706, via the notion of "perform a duty of respect toward." Related: *Honored*; *honoring*.

What does honor have to do with Venus and what you value, like or dislike? Value is also a noun and a verb!

value (n.)

c. 1300, "price equal to the intrinsic worth of a thing;" late 14c., "degree to which something is useful or estimable," from Old French *value* "worth, price, moral worth; standing, reputation" (13c.), noun use of fem. past participle of *valoir* "be worth," from Latin *valere* "be strong, be well; be of value, be worth" (from PIE root ***wal-** "to be strong"). The meaning "social principle" is attested from 1918, supposedly borrowed from the language of painting. *Value judgment* (1889) is a loan-translation of German *Werturteil*.

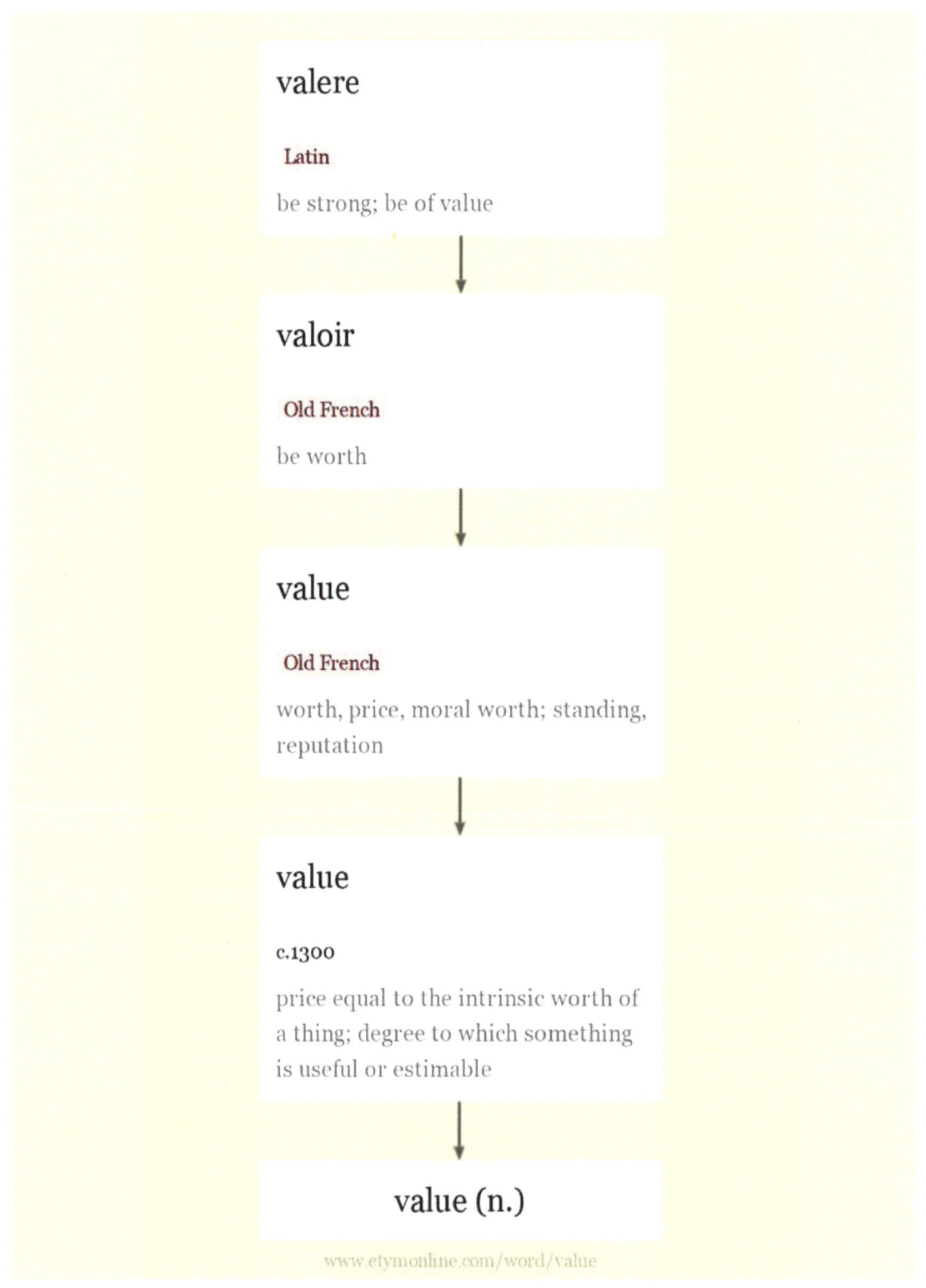

valere

Latin

be strong; be of value

valoir

Old French

be worth

value

Old French

worth, price, moral worth; standing, reputation

value

c.1300

price equal to the intrinsic worth of a thing; degree to which something is useful or estimable

value (n.)

www.etymonline.com/word/value

value (v.)

mid-15c., "estimate the value of," also "think highly of," probably from **value** (n.). Related: *Valued*, *valuing*.

What is intrinsic?

intrinsic (adj.)

late 15c., "interior, inward, internal," from Old French *intrinsèque* "inner" (14c.), from Medieval Latin *intrinsecus* "interior, internal," from Latin *intrinsecus* (adv.) "inwardly, on the inside," from *intra* "within" (see **intra-**) + *secus* "along, alongside," from PIE *sekw-os-* "following," suffixed form of root ***sekw-** (1) "to follow."
The form in English was conformed to words in *-ic* by 18c. Meaning "belonging to the nature of a thing" is from 1640s. Related: *Intrinsical*; *intrinsically*.

To follow alongside... with what? The internal! The self!
You are not to be led around by others! Take the info Mercury and then go to Venus and evaluate it and make a choice, then go to Mars and take action!

We are always being challenged by the spiritual spread
Why would the spirit challenge us knowing we are in chaos?
Because this is how you build character... the earth is school, and you are to learn by experiment which requires the 5 openness and the 4 breaking down to build up and the 2 cooperation with others and spirit!

WINNING FORMULA FOR HONORING YOURSELF

Spend time Communicating to the Self info from your environment
Do you know who YOU are? Get a PHD in you!
Establish what is yours and not yours
Let your yes be your yes and no, no
It's ok to change your mind, be flexible
Perception is not reality, it's personal
Stop tolerating what you don't like, your cells are suffering!

PEARLS OF WISDOM AND POWER MOMENT

Photo courtesy of Pexels.com by Ekaterina Bolovtsova

"SET THE ATMOSPHERE"

You tell people how to treat you by how you treat yourself. How you honor yourself. How you respect yourself. How you honor your word. You can wear all the crystals and burn all the sage and wear all the pearls but if you do not set the atmosphere in your internal environment, your external environment will always be a nightmare no matter how dreamy the outside looks.

<u>**September 20, 2022**</u>

<u>**Brand Image: Original or Copy?**</u>

Eric Thomas said It's a battle every single day to do what's right. Are you disciplined? This is chaos magic; this is the ability to go to the underworld and come out with the keys unscathed. This entire earth plane is the underworld, is it not? Do you not battle dos, don'ts, temptations, and choices every day? What is your viewpoint? What is your perspective? How do you choose to see things?

Here is the danger of a brand we trust. We only came to trust it because we were repeatedly told the same story over and over even if it was a lie until we believed it. Repetition makes a lie believable! Let me repeat that! Repetition makes a lie believable! Some of the most gifted salespeople have the gift of gab and can talk you right up out of your drawls! They know all the right notes to hit but if you look carefully at their life, there is little evidence of the things they say. Your brain cannot resist being told something over and over again. This is why you must be careful with other peoples suggestions to you because what you do becomes a part of your brand. What story are you telling yourself over and over? What story do you allow others to keep telling you?

My stance on what integrity looks like is not a popular one and I have come to be ok with it.

I don't believe in cutting corners and I believe in keeping my word.

I hear a lot of things in spirituality that at first seemed cool and freeing, but I now see as keeping a person limited.

How you do one thing, is how you do everything.

One of the things is quit your job. This is ludicrous because you need income.

The same habits you have when you work for someone else will be the same habits you have when you decide to work for you andddd they will actually be worse because you don't have anyone holding you accountable...

The return to work is going to increase as people see that entrepreneurship is not easier then working for someone else...

This is what chaos magic, and the underworld and Saturn are all about...

You can not have success in your light until you have success in your dark...

You will not get your rewards from Pluto and Saturn until you allow transformation and boundaries to have its work in you till you become mature in your thinking.

Most of us are living in the shadow of Neptune with the delusion that we can escape the work and results that come from what we do or don't do... no answer IS an answer! No action IS an action!

I have found several words related to brand image to help you have a firm understanding of what brand image is all about:

brand (n.)
Old English *brand, brond* "fire, flame, destruction by fire; firebrand, piece of burning wood, torch," and (poetic) "sword," from Proto-Germanic **brandaz* "a burning" (source also of Old Norse *brandr*, Old High German *brant*, Old Frisian *brond* "firebrand; blade of a sword," German *brand* "fire"), from PIE root ***gwher-** "to heat, warm." Meaning "iron instrument for branding" is from 1828. Meaning "mark made by a hot iron" (1550s), especially on a cask, etc., to identify the maker or quality of its contents, broadened by 1827 to marks made in other ways, then to "a particular make of goods" (1854). ***Brand-name*** is from 1889; ***brand-loyalty*** from 1961. Old French *brand, brant*, Italian *brando* "sword" are from Germanic (compare **brandish**).

brand (v.)

c. 1400, "to impress or burn a mark upon with a hot iron, cauterize; stigmatize," originally of criminal marks or cauterized wounds, from **brand** (n.). Figuratively, often in a bad sense, "fix a character of infamy upon," mid-15c., with the criminal marking in mind. As a means of marking ownership or quality of property, 1580s. Related: *Branded; branding*.

*gwher-
Proto-Indo-European root meaning "to heat, warm." It forms all or part of:
brand; **brandish**; **brandy**; **brimstone**; **brindled**; **forceps**; **Fornax**;
fornicate; **fornication**; **fornix**; **furnace**; **hypothermia**; **thermal**; **thermo-**;
Thermopylae; **Thermos**.
It is the hypothetical source of/evidence for its existence is provided by:
Sanskrit *gharmah* "heat;" Old Persian *Garmapada-*, name of the fourth month,
corresponding to June/July, from *garma-* "heat;" Hittite *war-* "to burn;"
Armenian *jerm* "warm;" Greek *thermos* "warm;" Latin *formus* "warm," *fornax*
"oven;" Old Irish *fogeir* "heated;" Old English *bærnan* "to kindle."

image (n.)

c. 1200, "piece of statuary; artificial representation that looks like a person or
thing," from Old French *image* "image, likeness; figure, drawing, portrait;
reflection; statue," earlier *imagene* (11c.), from Latin *imaginem* (nominative
imago) "copy, imitation, likeness; statue, picture," also "phantom, ghost,
apparition," figuratively "idea, appearance," from stem of *imitari* "to copy,
imitate" (from PIE root ***aim-** "to copy"). Meaning "reflection in a mirror" is
early 14c. The mental sense was in Latin and appears in English late 14c.
Sense of "public impression" is attested in isolated cases from 1908 but not in
common use until its rise in the jargon of advertising and public relations, c.
1958. To þe ymage of god he made hym [Genesis i.27, Wycliffite Bible, early
version, 1382]

image (v.)

late 14c., "to form a mental picture (of something), imagine," from Old French
imagier, from *image* (see **image** (n.)). Related: *Imaged; imaging*. ***aim-** Proto-
Indo-European root meaning "to copy." It forms all or part of: **emulate**;
emulation; **emulous**; **image**; **imaginary**; **imagination**; **imaginative**;
imagine; **imago**; **imitable**; **imitate**; **imitative**; **imitator**; **inimitable**. It is the
hypothetical source of/evidence for its existence is provided by: Latin *imago*
"image," *aemulus* "emulous," *imitari* "to copy, portray, imitate;" Hittite *himma-*
"imitation, substitute."

aim (v.)

c. 1300, "to estimate (number or size), calculate, count," senses now obsolete, from Old French *aesmer*, *esmer* (Old North French *amer*) "to value, rate; count, estimate," ultimately from Latin *aestimare* "appraise, determine the value of" (see **esteem** (v.)). The meaning in English apparently developed from "calculate," to "calculate with a view to action, plan," then to "direct a missile, a blow, etc." (late 14c.). It also was used in Middle English of directing a letter, planting an altar, pitching a tent. The intransitive sense of "intend, attempt" (early 14c.) was used by Shakespeare but is now considered colloquial. Related: *Aimed*; *aiming*.

aim (n.)

late 14c., "a purpose, thing intended;" from **aim** (v.) or from nouns from the verb in Old French. The meaning "action of aiming" is from early 15c. To **take aim** originally was *make aim* (early 15c.). **aimless (adj.)** "without aim or purpose," 1620s, from **aim** (n.) + **-less**. Related: *Aimlessly*; *aimlessness*.

Definitions of **aim** from WordNet

1

aim (v.)

point or cause to go (blows, weapons, or objects such as photographic equipment) towards;

Please don't **aim** at your little brother!

Synonyms: take / train / take aim / direct

aim (v.)

propose or intend;

I **aim** to arrive at noon

Synonyms: purpose / purport / propose

aim (v.)

move into a desired direction of discourse;

Synonyms: drive / get

aim (v.)

specifically design a product, event, or activity for a certain public;

Synonyms: calculate / direct

aim (v.)

intend (something) to move towards a certain goal;

He **aimed** his fists towards his opponent's face

Synonyms: <u>target</u> / <u>place</u> / <u>direct</u> / <u>point</u>

Original
*dhwer-
Proto-Indo-European root meaning "door, doorway." The base form is frequently in dual or plural, leading to speculation that houses of the original Indo-Europeans had doors with two swinging halves. It forms all or part of: **afforest**; **deforest**; **door**; **faubourg**; **foreclose**; **foreign**; **forensic**; **forest**; **forfeit**; **forum**; **hors d'oeuvre**; **thyroid**.
It is the hypothetical source of/evidence for its existence is provided by: Sanskrit *duárah* "door, gate;" Old Persian *duvara-* "door;" Lithuanian *dùrys* (plural); Greek *thyra* "door;" Latin *foris* "out-of-doors, outside;" Gaulish *doro* "mouth;" Old Prussian *dwaris* "gate;" Russian *dver'* "a door;" Old English *dor*, German *Tür* "door," Gothic *dauro* "gate."

Copy
*op-
Proto-Indo-European root meaning "to work, produce in abundance."
It forms all or part of: **cooperate**; **cooperation**; **copious**; **copy**; **cornucopia**; **hors d'oeuvre**; **inure**; **maneuver**; **manure**; **oeuvre**; **office**; **official**; **officinal**; **omni-**; **omnibus**; **omnium gatherum**; **op. cit.**; **opera**; **operate**; **operation**; **operose**; **optimism**; **optimum**; **opulence**; **opulent**; **opus**; **Oscan**.
It is the hypothetical source of/evidence for its existence is provided by: Sanskrit *apas-* "work, religious act," *apnas-* "possession, property;" Hittite *happina-* "rich;" Avestan *huapah-* "doing good work, masterly;" Latin *opus* "a work, labor, exertion;" Greek *ompne* "food, corn;" Old High German *uoben* "to start work, to practice, to honor;" German *üben* "to exercise, practice;" Dutch *oefenen,* Old Norse *æfa,* Danish *øve* "to exercise, practice;" Old English *æfnan* "to perform, work, do," *afol* "power."

copy (n.)
mid-14c., "written account or record," from Old French *copie* (13c.) and directly from Medieval Latin *copia* "reproduction, transcript," from Latin *copia* "an abundance, ample supply, profusion, plenty," from assimilated form of *com* "with" (see **com-**) + *ops* (genitive *opis*) "power, wealth, resources," from PIE root ***op-** "to work, produce in abundance." Sense extended 15c. to any specimen of writing, especially MS given to a printer to be reproduced in type (Caxton, late 15c.). Meaning "a duplication, imitation, or reproduction" written

or otherwise is from late 14c. Meaning "one of a set of reproductions containing the same matter" is from 1530s.

Copy-boy, one who takes copy from the writer to the printer, is from 1888. The newspaper *copy-desk*, where copy is edited for printing, is from 1887; *copy-editor* is attested from 1889. The "copy desk" is the managing editor's literary inspection field, his last check by which the work of all editorial departments is gauged, the final balance where the brain product of the entire working force of the paper is weighed and judged. [The Journalist, May 21, 1892]

copy (v.)

late 14c., "make a copy of, duplicate" (a text or document), from Old French *copier* (14c.) and directly from Medieval Latin *copiare* "to transcribe," originally "to write in plenty," from Latin *copia* "plenty" (see **copy** (n.)). Hence, "to write an original text many times." Figurative sense of "to imitate, to follow as an example" is attested from 1640s. Of computer data, by 1953. Meaning "send a copy (of a letter, later e-mail, etc.) to a third party" is attested by 1983. Related: *Copied*; *copying*.

*aim-

Proto-Indo-European root meaning "to copy."

It forms all or part of: **emulate**; **emulation**; **emulous**; **image**; **imaginary**; **imagination**; **imaginative**; **imagine**; **imago**; **imitable**; **imitate**; **imitative**; **imitator**; **inimitable**. It is the hypothetical source of/evidence for its existence is provided by: Latin *imago* "image," *aemulus* "emulous," *imitari* "to copy, portray, imitate;" Hittite *himma-* "imitation, substitute."

Identity

identity (n.)

c. 1600, "sameness, oneness, state of being the same," from French *identité* (14c.), from Medieval Latin *identitatem* (nominative *identitas*) "sameness," ultimately from Latin *idem* (neuter) "the same" (see **idem**). **idem (adv.)** "the same (as above)," used to avoid repetition in writing, Latin, literally "the same," from *id* "it, that one," from PIE pronominal stem **i-* (see **yon**) + demonstrative suffix *-dem*. **yon (adj., pron.)** Old English *geon* "that (over there)," from Proto-Germanic **jaino-* (source also of Old Frisian *jen*, Old Norse *enn*, Old High German *ener*, Middle Dutch *ghens*, German *jener*, Gothic *jains* "that, you"), from PIE pronominal stem **i-* (source also of Sanskrit *ena-*, third person pronoun, *anena* "that;" Latin *idem* "the same," *id* "it, that one;" Old Church Slavonic *onu* "he;" Lithuanian *ans* "he"). As an adverb from late 15c., a shortening of **yonder**. **idempotent (n.)** in algebra, quantity which multiplied by itself gives itself, 1870, from Latin *idem* "the same, identical with" (see **idem**) + *potentem* "powerful" (see **potent**). ***poti-** Proto-Indo-European root meaning "powerful; lord." It forms all or part of: **bashaw**; **compos mentis**; **despot**; **hospodar**; **host** (n.1) "person who receives guests;" **idempotent**; **impotent**; **omnipotent**; **pasha**; **plenipotentiary**; **posse**; **possess**; **possible**; **potence**; **potency**; **potent**; **potentate**; **potential**; **potentiate**; **potentiometer**; **power**; **totipotent**. It is the hypothetical source of/evidence for its existence is provided by: Sanskrit *patih* "master, husband;" Greek *posis*, Lithuanian *patis* "husband;" Latin *potis* "powerful, able, capable; possible."

Notice that root word of image and copy both have aim "to copy in abundance" as their root word!

Your brand is not WHO you are, it's what you do… Your name, a name is not who you are either… it's what you do! Your brand is not your logo or your mantra, it's your REPUTATION what you are known for … overtime! What you repeatedly do!

Your breath gives you the power in this life to take action. If you are breathing you can take action. And no action is still an action! The breath is why you exist! It's why you are here!

The process of creating the body in Hebrew means a body powerfully rolled together that was really hard to do! It was not easy making your avatar! It's complex! The breath is not so! It's the word yasar and means to squeezed or stress into shape. You were not made to be in your body. Your body is a constraint on unlimited potential! (See Genesis 2:7 and Psalm 139:13-16)

Jesus is not a noun but a verb that means to save, to give victory to
The word Lord is havaw and means to breathe
Christ in the Greek means to gape the mouth, to yawn
Spirit is the Hebrew root word for psycho which means to breathe
Soul in Hebrew is nawfash and means to breathe
Psyche in the Greek means breath, life, soul

So we see all these things mean breath which is life. "Lord Jesus" is **a saying** that literally means to **breath victory**. Breathe victory on who? You through your body. It was demanding work putting you together! Use your body as the vehicle it's meant to be for the breath, the life that's in you! Wasting your body is wasting your breath!

WHO you are does not come from your brand or your identity or the image you copied which all comes from your programming and your conditioning. Who you are is also not all your gifts talents and abilities. That is just what you do. If you are breathing that means a lot. It means you are here for a reason and that is purpose. It's up to you to discover what you must do now that you know WHO you are which is the breath. You should first and foremost identify with spirit and things of the spirit. Presence creates possibility. That fact that you have breath in your body means anything is possible. You have a blank canvas. Stop resisting and start existing. Just breathe.

Without the breath, you would cease to exist! Death is unconsciousness. When you are not aware of your existence, you are literally the walking dead. When you are not aware of the power of your own existence, you need the energy of others being unaware of your own existence. **You are only you when you are aware of your breath**. The awareness of your breath. The act of breathing. That is consciousness. That is who you are. A breathing avatar. And your avatar has purpose, you are the ethnicity you are, height, weight, shape, color, gender, etc for a specific purpose that was chosen before you got here! Also, Emotions are not bad. They are indicators. That fact that you feel is an awareness that you are breathing. Acknowledge your emotions and learn how to deal with them. The only people who no longer FEEL anything are people whose breath has left them, and their avatar no longer walks among us. So don't despise the body! Don't despise your avatar! You need it! Your breath needs it! Your brands needs it!

Look at the definitions for the words brand and identity again. Notice that brand means to put a mark on, but identity is about the mark within! 🏛

You can find what is called brand knockoffs anywhere. This is where someone puts on a mark or a name of a well-known brand on an inferior product. And if you are not careful, to the untrained eye, they look the same.

I can put the brand name of Coach on a Walmart purse but that does not make it a Coach bag. You will be able to tell in THE WAY that it FUNCTIONS.

When I used to buy Walmart purses, I also had to replace them a couple times a year. I thought I was saving money but when I added up what I was spending it was the same amount as a medium size Coach bag!

When I bought my first Coach bag, I thought why am I doing this and then after going a whole 2 years and not one tear in my bag, I understood why brand image is important. I will never buy a cheap bag again!

Inferior products may look "powerfully put together" but they are dead! They have no life in them! They have no breath and leave you wanting for more. Your body is put together powerfully but if you don't put some quality inside of you... if you don't spend some time building your brand image to last, you are like the walking dead!

A lot of people fail in life because they have a BRAND, they created a name, put a name on themselves, but it's not their true identity! They are a fake! And slowly it will be revealed that they **aimed** at making a copy of an original!

Talk is cheap! Calling something by a different name will not change the way it functions. An identity is of itself, it's intrinsic, the quality is within, not without! I can decide to call a cat a dog, but it will never bark like a dog can!

A Brand is created. It's your reputation. Its the result of all the things you put together. A reputation is built over time. It's what other people come to think about you. Not what they say, what they think. Everything you do is either helping your brand or hurting your brand.

Identity is either rights or duty oriented. It is also cultural as well, subject to programming. Rights are a demand for a reward and duty should not seek rewards. Your identity is a group of patterns whether productive or destructive. Identity is endless work shifting patterns for the better. The self is fluid. We need to move from Ego to Consciousness.

We know what Ego is but what is consciousness?

Consciousness
*ane-
Proto-Indo-European root meaning "to breathe."
It forms all or part of: **anemo-**; **anemometer**; **anemone**; **anima**; **animadversion**; **animadvert**; **animal**; **animalcule**; **animalistic**; **animate**; **animation**; **animatronic**; **anime**; **animism**; **animosity**; **animus**; **Enid**; **equanimity**; **longanimity**; **magnanimous**; **pusillanimous**; **unanimous**. It is the hypothetical source of/evidence for its existence is provided by: Sanskrit *aniti* "breathes;" Greek *anemos* "wind;" Latin *animus* "rational soul, mind, life, mental powers, consciousness, sensibility; courage, desire," *anima* "living being, soul, mind, disposition, passion, courage, anger, spirit, feeling;" Old Irish *anal*, Welsh *anadl* "breath," Old Irish *animm* "soul;" Gothic *uzanan* "to exhale," Old Norse *anda* "to breathe," Old English *eðian* "to breathe;" Old Church Slavonic *vonja* "smell, breath;" Armenian *anjn* "soul."

consciousness (n.)
1630s, "internal knowledge," from **conscious** + **-ness**. Meaning "state of being aware of what passes in one's own mind" is from 1670s; meaning "state of being aware" of anything is from 1746. *Consciousness-raising* is attested from 1968.

Ahhhh! So we see that consciousness means that one is animated, breathing, a state of being aware of the thoughts that comes in and out of one's mind. It means this person is not just skipping through the fields with their head in the clouds like the fools journey on the zero Tarot deck card. They are alive and life is shown as they are moving with purpose. Are you moving according to your purpose? Are you animated and breathing? Are you aware of what passes through your mind and why? What is your brand image?

WINNING FORMULA FOR BEING AN ORIGINAL

So what's the winning formula for creating a brand image that is original and not a copy?

First become aware that all you are is the breath. Anything is possible at this point. You exist right now in this moment and that is your power.

Understand your brand is not who you are. It is what you do and what you do comes from your programming and your conditioning.

Your brand is your reputation and reputation is built over time by repeating the same behaviors. This is what people trust you do, good or bad.

Learn how to use the ego to remain confident within but unaffected without. This only happens when you train your responses to life. Key word here is train.

Realize that no one's is you and that that is power too! They can copy, **aim** to be you but they are not you! Don't let the fact that people unaware of their power copying you stop you from building your brand or change who you fundamentally are on the inside!

PEARL OF WISDOM AND POWER MOMENT

Photo courtesy of Pexels.com by Antony Trivet

"IN TO ME SEE"

Who are you? Do you know who you are? Have you spent time getting intimate with you? You cannot build a solid image without first knowing what you are made of from the inside out. This will require you to come away from asking other people their opinion as they can only speak from their own brand image which may not align with yours. You can only effectively evaluate an outside opinion of your brand image once you understand who you are from within.

October 11th, 2022

The Process of Character

I decided to add an energy update in my rooms to demonstrate how the room message I get from spirit aligns with the energy of the cosmos. Enjoy!

Energy update: 4 ♣, 10/18/2022 (16/7), The sun in Libra 24* ♎, squaring the Moon in Cancer 29* ☺

The 4 is ruled by Uranus and is all about tearing down and innovating. It's rebellious and goes against the status quo. The 16/7 with the 7 being ruled by Neptune is the moment of impact, the moment of rude awakening. It is the Tower card in the Tarot deck. The potential for evil is strong with this number but those with righteous character can overcome with glory and victory. The power to overcome requires deep introspection and tapping into your spiritual gifts and set boundaries like the 12 th beckons us to before we move into Aries ♈ I am... you must check your Pisces, I believe, which is what do you believe, before you can move into your I AM Aries 1st house.

WHO you are in relationships behind closed doors is having difficulty with how you feel internally about those private relationships and how you display those feelings publicly. Who you are and what you do are at odds with each other! The inside and the outside do not match! This is due to a character flaw! The moon is at a critical degree in Leo! Why is it critical? Because your feelings about your private life are on a public stage putting on a show right now and the sun at a Pisces degree wants you to keep your personality under wraps and be quiet about who you really are, that is Neptune delusion, rose colored glasses but this cannot be. Mercury is in Libra at 10 degrees which is Capricorn, and you need forget about your feelings and speak your truth about the relationships you are in with other people. Uranus in Taurus 17* is Leo again telling you to go public with your personal preferences and your individuality and you may be seen as a rebel for doing so! You are gonna have to be ok with doing that! Pluto in cap 26* is transforming your values and those things you hold dear and the way you go about working to achieve your goals. Jupiter is just barely getting started in Aries so baby steps with the actions outwardly. It's retrograde so this means expansion within before expansion without. Oddly enough, Chiron in Aries 13*, NN in Taurus 14*, and MC in Pisces 24* are all here to help with that internal process. NN wants you to go within and question your comfort and security and the things you value, Chiron wants you to deal with those wounds of the self that stop you from taking action on internal change... You been hearing from Spirit that you need to change your ways, so this is the time to do it. If you do the internal work and grow deep roots within now, in other words let life teach you 👊🏽 you will be able to weather the storms as we descend into the underworld during this winter season. If you do the work, you will be ready and well equipped to take firm action come spring!

Today Saturn is at 18* which is Virgo in Aquarius... retrograde... this is shadow work, a lengthy process using the occult sciences to discover the internal work that needs to be done. Neptune is also at 23* that's Aquarius in Pisces ♓ retrograde. Again taking off those rose-colored glasses and saying I know and not I believe anymore. What is it that you really know about yourself and your spiritual practices when you are alone in that 12 th house comfortable at home to let your hair down? Who are you truly in private?

Let's look at how to stand tall and integrate the shadow work to build your character like the bamboo does:

bamboo (n.)
type of giant grass common in the tropics, 1590s, from Dutch *bamboe* and/or Portuguese *bambu*, earlier *mambu* (16c.), probably from Malay (Austronesian) *samambu*, though some suspect this is itself an imported word, perhaps from Kanarese (Dravidian). ***Bamboo curtain*** in reference to communist China (based on ***iron curtain***) is from 1949.

samambu means you were born somewhere around the territory of ***Central India*** approximately in ***1850***. Your profession was ***philosopher and thinker***. Psychologically, you were timid, constrained, and quiet. You had creative talents, waited until that life to be liberated. Sometimes environment considered you strange. Your main task - to make the world more beautiful. Physical and spiritual deserts are just waiting for your touch. Keep smiling!

This words *samambu* is a kind of rattan, which was used as a walking-stick, and which was called the Malacca cane by the English comes from the Native American word that means walking stick!

So them bamboo is a walking stick and embodies all the aspects of the walking stick which shows you how to build character!

Here is an online article about walking sticks:
https://seekadventuresblog.com/5-reasons-to-use-a-walking-stick/

According to the article, the five reasons a person should use a walking stick are to develop what is called "Trail cred," stability, endurance, safety, and swag. Trail cred reminded me of street cred. You can always tell when someone is not from the hood. They don't look like anyone from there and they are not wearing the right stuff. When I go back to my hometown, I don't wear flashy colors and I don't wear excessive jewelry. I look the part of someone from the hood. Looking the part gives you street cred and using a walking stick on a trail let's others know you know where you at and what you are doing.

Trail Cred: Do you have the right tools/skills for the job
Stability:What support system do you have to lean on in times of trouble
Endurance: You cannot go alone all the way; you need tools to keep you going!
Safety: The gardener knows how to turn his garden tools into a weapon when needed 💯
Swag: Celebrate all the trails you have endured and overcome

Wikipedia definition of a walking stick:
as a support when going uphill or as a brake when going downhill; as a balance point when crossing streams, swamps, or other rough terrain; to feel for obstacles in the path; to test mud and water for depth; to enhance the cadence of striding, and as a defence against animals. 17/18 century used to display social status to distinguish their status and wealth and as self defense. used by both western and eastern Christian churches.[2][3] In Islam the walking stick ('Asa) is considered a sunnah and Muslims are encouraged to carry one. The imam traditionally delivers the Khutbah while leaning on a stick.[4] Bamboos are sometimes popularly distinguished (after a native idiom) as male and female; the latter embracing all the common species with hollow stems, the former title being applied to a certain kind (in fact, of a distinct genus, *Dendrocalamus strictus*), which has a solid or nearly solid core, and is much used for bludgeons and spear-shafts ie weapons...

Now what is interesting is that walking sticks are made of study material to last such as bamboo. Let's look at what bamboo and walking sticks have in common.

The bamboo is a strong 💪 material. We call it a tree, but it is really just tall grass that took 5 years to grow. Why so long? Because underneath it is building an intricate root system that goes wide and deep and is so interconnected with the earth that it protects itself from soil erosion and has the best water retention and drainage system. When the first leaves grow as they get older they shield the baby ones and the baby ones spread out so that some of the elder leaves get sunlight. As tough as bamboo is, it bends when storms come! It yields! That is receptive, feminine energy at work! It is able to bend because it took time to develop on the inside before it grew in the public eye! You can only yield when you know who you are on the inside.

Rhizomes are used to store starches and proteins and enable plants to perennate (survive an annual unfavorable season) underground. They are also asexual able to produce by themselves!The following plants and herbs are examples of rhizomes: **hops, asparagus, ginger, irises, lily of the valley, cannas, and sympodial orchids**.

What can you produce without anyones help? This requires deep roots, deep work under the surface where no one can see!

Now let's look at an animal that has similar characteristics like the bamboo:

Eagle

*awi-
Proto-Indo-European root meaning "bird." It also might be the source of **woyo, *oyyo*, Proto-Indo-European words for "egg." Sanskrit *vih*, Avestan *vish*, Latin *avis* "bird;" Greek *aietos* "eagle;" Old Church Slavonic *aja*, Russian *jajco*, Breton *ui*, Welsh *wy*, Greek *ōon*, Latin *ovum*, Old Norse *egg*, Old High German *ei*, Gothic *ada* all meaning "egg."

eagle (n.)
"very large diurnal raptorial bird of the genus *Aquila*," mid-14c., from Old French *egle*, from Old Provençal *aigla*, from Latin *aquila* "black eagle," fem. of

aquilus "eagle," often explained as "the dark colored" (bird); see **aquiline**. The native term was **erne**.

Golf score sense is by 1908 (according to old golf sources, because it "soars higher" than a **birdie**). As the name of a U.S. $10 coin minted from 1792 to 1933, established in the 1786 resolution for a new monetary system (but at first only the desperately needed small copper coins were minted). The figurative ***eagle-eyed*** "sharp-sighted" (like an eagle) is attested from c. 1600.

Bald
Sanskrit *bhalam* "brightness, forehead , from PIE root ***bhel-** (1) "to shine, flash, gleam"

Aquila

northern constellation, late 14c., from Latin *aquila* "eagle" (see **aquiline**). Latin *aquila* often is explained as "the dark bird;" compare *aquilus* "blackish, swarthy, of the color of darkness," but some suggest the color word is from the bird. De Vaan writes, "It is possible that 'eagle' was derived from *aquilus* 'dark' when this had received its colour meaning. It may not be the only dark bird, but it is certainly one of the biggest and most majestic of them." As for *aquilus*, "The Romans derived this colour from *aqua* 'water', which [Etymologicum Magnum] reject because they cannot imagine water being black. Still, this seems a more likely derivation to me than from *aquila* 'eagle' ...."

Mercury

"the Roman god Mercury," herald and ambassador of his father, Jupiter, mid-12c., *Mercurie*, from Latin *Mercurius* "Mercury," originally a god of tradesmen and thieves, from *merx* "merchandise" (see **market** (n.)); or perhaps [Klein, Tucker] from Etruscan and influenced by *merx*. De Vaan thinks it possible the whole stem **merk-* was borrowed and the god-name with it.

Mercury later was identified with Greek Hermes and still later with Germanic Woden. From his role as a messenger and conveyor of information, since mid-17c. *Mercury* has been a common name for a newspaper.

The planet closest to the sun was so called in classical Latin (c. 1300 in English). A hypothetical inhabitant of the planet was a *Mercurean* (1855) or a *Mercurian* (1755). For the metallic element, see **mercury**.

In U.S. numismatics, the ***Mercury-head dime*** (so called by 1941) was in circulation from 1916; properly it is the female head of Liberty, in her characteristic cap, here winged to symbolize freedom of thought. But the

resemblance to Mercury was noted in coin circles at once, and the coin design sometimes was popularly mistaken as the head of Mercury, Roman god of making money and thieving, in his winged hat. It was so-called in 1933 in newspaper articles calling attention to the fasces on the reverse. The coin is more correctly the *Winged Liberty-head dime* (simple *Liberty-head dime* being a designation of the previous design). The design was replaced in 1946, which made it necessary for it to have an agreed-upon specifying name.
There's the four-year-old who counted out 20 cents with the remark: "A boy dime and a girl dime.Translated, this means a Roosevelt dime and one classified by coin books as the "new Mercury head" dime.
[Dothan Eagle, June 25, 1951]

erne (n.)

"sea eagle," from Old English *earn* "eagle," from Proto-Germanic **aron-, *arnuz* "eagle" (source also of Old High German *arn*, German *Aar*, Middle Dutch *arent*, Old Norse *örn*, Gothic *ara* "eagle"), from PIE root **or-* "great bird" (source also of Greek *ornis* "bird," Old Church Slavonic *orilu*, Lithuanian *erelis*, Welsh *eryr* "eagle"). The Germanic word also survives in the first element of names such as **Arnold** and **Arthur**.

The name Arnold is a masculine **German, Dutch and English** given name. It is composed of the Germanic elements arn "eagle" and wald "power, brightness".

Arthur means **believed to be derived from the word "artos," meaning "bear." As experts differ on its precision origin, the name can also mean "Thor, the eagle" and "strong man."** Arthur became a popular choice during the Middle Ages, as families named their boys after King Arthur of 6th century England.

So what do the bamboo and the eagle have to do with each other? They both take time to build their inner world, their character.Along with the bear, they are the strongman.

Eagle is a 4 ♡ in Cardology, and Bamboo is 9 ♣, Bear is King of ♠, Scorpio is 4 ♣ which fails in the moon, has a detriment in Venus, and exaltation in Uranus... the bear is the symbol of Russia 9 ♡ and they are known not to show very much emotions so this is fitting because the 9 is all about conclusions and the heart is emotions, so the conclusion of emotions. A bear does not show out publicly unless angered and the King of Spades ♠ has mastered their emotions along with their intellect and value system.

The Eagle is the 4 ♡ which is restructuring the home with continuous renewal, this is your ability to not give up when it seems like a storm is brewing and you can't hear spirit talking to you. The bear has mastered it all and must use its gifts wisely, must be mature with its power. Scorpio is the debate, but it is the debate with self. It's you against you. Only you know the secrets you hold within and only you can do the work to be truly free inside and out.

The bamboo goes deep like Scorpio. It is not worried about surface level things; it knows it's a given and does not care about its own comfort or security like Venus does. Venus is a problem for Scorpio because Mars and Pluto don't care what you like! The 9 works with the zero so you can become the 1 again! The 9 is about service to humanity and you need strength of character, you must go then the process of character to truly serve from the heart.

The story of the eagle going through transformation (which some deem to be false) at the age of 40 where it sits and breaks it's own beak and then plucks out it's own feathers and then sits and waits for those things to grow back has turned out to be false! Lol 😆 If the eagle did that it would die!

The eagle does go thru a process of molting twice a year and it's talons and beak are constantly being renewed like your fingernails break and grow back... it's a continuous lifetime renewal. It does live to be 70 but 7 is a spiritual number ruled by Neptune which rules Pisces ♓ and that zero is the 12 th house the womb of creation where everything fades away and you come out a new creation, a new person (Aries).

This has more to do with the myth of the Phoenix which makes a nest of cinnamon and sets itself on fire in it's own nest, and then is reborn from the ashes... this is a symbol of regeneration... oddly enough our bodies regenerate and become new every 7 years... there goes the seven again!

The Greek historian Herodotus is credited with introducing the legend of the phoenix into Western culture after his travels in Egypt. The earliest representation of the phoenix is found in the ancient Egyptian **Bennu** bird, the name relating to the verb "weben," meaning "to rise brilliantly," or "to shine." Some researchers believe that a now extinct large heron was a possible real-life inspiration for the Bennu. But there is a real bird called the Queztal in qautemala that looks like the mythical Phoenix. The birds name means sacred, divine and is a symbol for the snake God in Mexico Quetzalcoatl. This is also kundalini rising, illumination.

WINNING FORMULA FOR DEVELOPING YOUR CHARACTER

Don't give up because you're not an overnight success. The bamboo takes 5 years before exponential growth!
Go deep! Sit with yourself and go beyond surface level question and really get to the heart of the matter. Take your time to Make your foundation strong 💪
Death and rebirth is a continual, lifetime process, not a major catastrophic event lol castrophic events, tower moments come from ignoring the renewal process and putting it off when there have been signs you need to change! Lol
Be honorable with your power, power is not always combative, the bamboo has more tensil strength then steel but yet it bends and yields during a storm, that's the secret to it surviving the storm and remaining rooted and not being broken.

It's stage time! 😃 (This is when I normally call people to the stage to have a group discussion... my favorite part!)

PEARL OF WISDOM AND POWER MOMENT

Photo courtesy of Pexels.com by Engin Akyurt

"TREASURES WITHIN"

Don't you know that your treasures are inside of you? Nothing outside of you can give you the satisfaction that having developed a good name and good character has. A pearl doesn't develop overnight, nor does it develop in a friendly environment. A pearl is the result of learning to protect oneself from the hostilities and irritations of life. When you take the time to develop your character, you will create something beautiful that is lasting and full of value.

November 15th, 2022

Trust: Who Do You Love?

Energy Update:

Sun 23* Scorpio ♏ Moon 11* Leo ♌ Mars 23* Gemini Retro ♊
North Node 12* Taurus ♉ Chiron 12* Aries ♈
11/15/2022 = 14/5, 6 day, Tuesday
5 ♣ day, Trust and Deceit are both a 7 ♣, Lies 6 ♣

The sun moon and mars all have Aquarius traits! This is disruption in the form of individuality and innovation. Mars is our desires and the actions we take but it's retrograde which means action on you internally not outwardly and it's in Gemini ♊ so it wants to see both sides and use both! Gemini can be seen as fickle, but Gemini knows it has the right to change its mind! Your personality is the sun, your conditioning is the moon, are all needing an overhaul, a do over from the inside out! The north node is like the moon in May that said do your internal work, and the last lunar eclipse asked for the receipts because now it's time to make your dreams a reality in the 12th house, let's build with what we got! Chiron joins the party and says let's go already and heal these self wounds and it's in Aries ♈ the planet of action and war... go to war on those parts of your personality and condition that no longer serve you and build something greater this time!

Can you trust yourself to do the work?

Who can you trust? What is trust? Let's talk about what is the opposite of trust first.

Distrust : to doubt the honesty or reliability of (intuition, gut feeling)

Mistrust: to have no confidence in (seeing patterns)

distrust (v.)

early 15c., "have a doubt or dread of" **dis-** word-forming element of Latin origin meaning 1. "lack of, not, in a different direction, between". The etymologically correct form is *mistrust*, in which both elements are Teutonic"

mistrust (n.)

"lack of confidence, suspicion, doubt, regard with jealousy or suspicion" mis means in a changed manner, PIE *mit-to-*, from root ***mei-** (1) "to change."

Distrust, you know something is off, but you are not sure 🤫. Mistrust is when you've seen or heard something that challenged what you thought you knew... you are not crazy! You heard what you heard, and you saw what you saw!

What is a Teutonic personality?
The Teutons (Germans) disclose **more strength and persistency of desire than the Celts.** Their feelings were slower, less impulsive; also less quickly diverted, more unswerving, and even fiercer in their strength. The general characteristic of Teutonic emotion is its close connection with some motive grounded in rational purpose.

Are your emotions grounded when it comes to this individual? Does it make sense? Is it a level playing field?
No ground rules or terms? Yeah, that is so they can keep switching and swerving on you!
But you scream, I want my freedom, I don't like being restrained! We all have Saturn in our chart! Freedom requires accountability and responsibility!

What does it mean to be free?

freedom (n.)

Old English *freodom* "power of self-determination, state of free will; emancipation from slavery, deliverance;" see **free** (adj.) + **-dom**. Meaning "exemption from arbitrary or despotic control, civil liberty" is from late 14c. Meaning "possession of particular privileges" is from 1570s. Similar formation in Old Frisian *fridom*, Dutch *vrijdom*, Middle Low German *vridom*.

free (adj.)

Old English *freo* "exempt from; not in bondage, acting of one's own will," also "noble; joyful," from Proto-Germanic **friaz* "beloved; not in bondage" (source also of Old Frisian *fri*, Old Saxon *vri*, Old High German *vri*, German *frei*, Dutch *vrij*, Gothic *freis* "free"), from PIE **priy-a-* "dear, beloved," from root ***pri-** "to love."
"clear of obstruction" is from mid-13c.; sense of "unrestrained in movement"

A truly free person does not set rules regulations and restrictions deadlines etc on you , they allow you to do you while they do them... the rules don't apply to them, but it applies to you? Red flag ▷

Ok what is trust?

Trust
c. 1200, "reliance on the veracity, integrity, or other virtues of someone or something; religious faith," from Old Norse *traust* "help, confidence, protection, support," from Proto-Germanic abstract noun **traustam* (source also of Old Frisian *trast*, Dutch *troost* "comfort, consolation," Old High German *trost* "trust, fidelity," German *Trost* "comfort, consolation," Gothic *trausti* "agreement, alliance"), from Proto-Germanic **treuwaz*, source of Old English *treowian* "to believe, trust," and *treowe* "faithful, trusty," from PIE root ***deru-** "be firm, solid, steadfast."
from c. 1300 as "reliability, trustworthiness; trustiness, fidelity, faithfulness;" from late 14c. as "confident expectation" and "that on which one relies." From early 15c. in legal sense of "confidence placed in a one who holds or enjoys the use of property entrusted to him by its legal owner;" mid-15c. as "condition of being legally entrusted." Meaning "businesses organized to reduce competition" is recorded from 1877. *Trust-buster* is recorded from 1903.

*deru-

also **dreu-*, Proto-Indo-European root meaning "be firm, solid, steadfast," with specialized senses "wood," "tree" and derivatives referring to objects made of wood such as oak.

What is special about the oak tree is that it is regarded as the most durable hardwood, and it is anti fungal. The main cause of fungal infection is compromised immunity!

A popular treatment for compromised immunity is gene 🧬 therapy! You got compromised because you changed your EXPRESSION, YOUR GENES 🧬 to fit someone's else narrative! You started acting out of your character!

Immunity has to do with Trust, compromised immunity means you are not free to be yourself in the relationship, partnership, etc and you must do what the other person wants or their behavior towards you changes when you don't do what they secretly want you to do (no ground rules, expectations were discussed)

I had to keep watch on my own immunity! People were trying to get me to change MY GENE 🧬 EXPRESSION to fit their narrative not too long ago. All at the SAME time, numerous people were getting at me to collaborate... it was overwhelming! Where were all these people when it was only me and my husband in the room? Like Drake said in his song *Over* that "I know way too many people here right now that I didn't know last year, who the F are y'all??!" LOL! Question number one, who has been there before the fame? Why was I so "popular" to collaborate with all of a sudden? My room was out there in the ethers and there were people who didn't have the audience size that I had! KNOW YOUR WORTH!!!!! I see soooo many people following people on this app who has done me dirty behind closed doors... but I don't go around telling tales! I am seeing wickedness in high places! Not low but High places!

Ephesians 6:12 For we wrestle not against flesh and blood, but against principalities, against powers, against the rulers of the darkness of this world, against spiritual **wickedness in high *places***.

Principalities
the person or thing that commences, the first person or thing in a series, the leader **archḗ,** ar-khay it starts with alpha...

This is the Alef in Hebrew, the ox, their objective is to get you to carry their burden, do their work!

Powers:
the power of authority (influence) and of right (privilege) ἐξουσία **exousía,** ex-oo-see'-ah; (in the sense of ability); privilege, i.e. (subjectively) force, capacity, competency, freedom, or (objectively) mastery (concretely,

magistrate, superhuman, potentate, token of control), delegated influence:—authority, jurisdiction, liberty, power, right, strength.

These people have influence! Influence is power! They know people and people know them or those people *think* they know them!
Jeremiah 3:2
Lift up thine eyes unto the **high places** and see where thou hast not been **lien** with. **In the ways hast thou sat for them**, as the Arabian in the wilderness; and thou hast polluted the land with thy whoredoms and with thy wickedness.

Here is the Hebrew breakdown of the key words in that verse above:

High place: שְׁפִי **sh^ephîy,** shef-ee'; bareness; concretely, a bare hill or plain:—high place, stick out. to be wind-swept, be bare, be scraped barren (by wind)

Lien: shaw-gal'; a primitive root; to copulate with:—lie with, ravish.

In what ways: daw-rak' , marching, journey of a distance! How far were you willing to go for them? Go to war for them? Compromise yourself, your gene 🧬 expression for them?

Sat for them: yaw-shab', abode dwelling! You were house sitting for them while they were away

In short, you have taken yourself to bed with these people in the wide open so they know you will look like a fool to separate yourself! This is how they trap you by causing you to go public with them from the beginning! Be mindful of how fast someone comes to you with something... they have an agenda to make an Alef, I mean an Ox out of you! I had to learn this the hard way!

Who are these people trying to get you to change your gene expression? WHO ARE THESE PEOPLE???

Rulers
κοσμοκράτωρ **kosmokrátōr,** kos-mok-rat'-ore; from G2889 and G2902; a world-ruler, an epithet of **Satan**:—ruler.

epithet (n.) "descriptive name for a person or thing,"

Spiritual wickedness

Pnyoo-mat-ik-os', pon-ay-ree'-ah 1 relating to the human spirit, or rational soul, as part of the man which is akin to God and serves as his instrument or organ that which possesses the nature of the rational soul

1. belonging to a spirit, or a being higher than man but inferior to God
2. belonging to the Divine Spirit... but have evil purposes and desires, from their depravity their habit of doing harm due to their dejection, their unhappy condition!

Sat for them: yaw-shab', abode dwelling!

You were house sitting for those rulers ie wicked people (twisted in their thinking) while they were away ! They are getting you to do their dirty work and take the fall for it!

HOW TO KNOW SOMEONE CAN'T BE TRUSTED

This is what I've noticed people do:
They act exclusive... play the chase me game
They use terms of endearment when they come to you
They use you to make others jealous to stir up desire for that "spot"
They play dumb "Whatchu meannnnn?" (Onset of confusion, self doubt)
Play on your emotions, They say it's you or that it's me (you're not good enough or I'm not good enough)
There are ALWAYS flags from the beginning (behavior/patterns)

WINNING FORMULA FOR VETTING SOMEONE

First of all, know your personal rules and boundaries

Are you just following the crowd and are you sure you have all the facts?

Is there a feeling of missing out or pressure to act fast?

Has there been a discussion of purpose and ground rules? (if not, red flag)

Who's benefiting here? Is it beneficial to BOTH parties?

"I like to just flow, no rules etc, red flag ▷

Does it serve a legitimate purpose & is the terms of the purpose (law) RELATED to the purpose?

Does this further your purpose, goal, dream, intention for your life? or just theirs???

Does it make sense? Do they just come out of the blue or from left field with their suggestion? It is reasonable?

Not everything is about cost and benefits! Killing someone to get insurance money to pay your bills is wrong and not rational anddddd breaks laws no matter what justification you can bring! If a hungry person who never stole before decides to steal a loaf of bread out of hunger will still pay the penalty if caught! There is a better way!

How did you get here! Nobody supposed to be here! Lol don't get swept up in a whirl of emotion

PEARL OF WISDOM AND POWER MOMENT

Photo courtesy of Pexels.com by Nara Meas

"PICTURE PERFECT"

The deceiver knows how to paint a pretty picture to make you fall head over heels. It's okay to vet someone first to make sure they are who they say they are. People pretend well and looks can be deceiving. It is never something unfamiliar as they would put you off from the start. It is always something or someone close to you, it's never a stranger. Remember that.

December 6th, 2022

Truth is: The Story of Truth

Energy Update:
12/06/2022 = 15/6 Tuesday Mars day

Q ♣ Queenly Communication, Critical Thinking
The Q is the 12 card… 4 queens x12= 48. This is foundation, innovation, and manifestation how by tearing down stinking thinking and clubs are wands in tarot which mean action. It sits Mercury Mars the 3rd, 6th, 1st house. This is the intellect, habits, routine, work, and just getting started already! Mercury is quick to move, and Mars is quick to fight! The Queen is challenged by all the choices she must make between family the 4 and her dreams the 8. This requires emotional intelligence. It also sits in the line of transpluto so constant transformations in movement and internal motives. Don't let all that sunshine go to your head queen, don't become vain with your Venus the 6! It's ok to pamper yourself but at some point you must get back to work! You want to have options and that can't happen if you are not using your good business sense, judgment, and communication skills!
Mars opposition the Sun on Thursday brighter then all the stars in the sky! Aries is exalted in the Sun! Desire Drive Motivation? Where is your Mars! Where is your Aries? Its going to show up big and bright this week! What does this mean? Mars thinks it's shining on its own, but it is just reflecting all that glorious light from the sun! Your motives, your desires, the things that drive you all come from your personality! What is your sign sign? It shines the light on your mars! Your personality is the reason why you do what you do, improve on it but never apologize for who you are meant to be!

If you want to know and better understand your placements in numerology, Cardology, astrology and even human design, I do readings and you may book by clicking the link up top and schedule your reading with me. I also offer coaching packages & consultation clarity sessions to get answers to nagging question or help solving a problem. Also I am currently open for New Year planning with my 2-hour virtual Vision Board Party where I help you strategize your entire year step by step! You will walk away with mantras, affirmations, words of power, and more all unique to you to help you get results for the year ahead.

truth (n.)
Old English *triewð* (West Saxon), *treowð* (Mercian) "faith, faithfulness, fidelity, loyalty; veracity, quality of being true; pledge, covenant," from Germanic abstract noun **treuwitho*, from Proto-Germanic *treuwaz* "having or characterized by good faith," from PIE **drew-o-*, a suffixed form of the root ***deru-** "be firm, solid, steadfast." With Germanic abstract noun suffix **-itho* (see **-th** (2)).
Sense of "something that is true" is first recorded mid-14c. Meaning "accuracy, correctness" is from 1560s. English and most other IE languages do not have a primary verb for "speak the truth," as a contrast to **lie** (v.). *Truth squad* in U.S. political sense first attested in the 1952 U.S. presidential election campaign.

betroth (v.)
c. 1300, *betrouthen*, "to promise to marry (a woman)," from **be-**, here probably with a sense of "thoroughly," + Middle English *treowðe* "truth," from Old English *treowðe* "truth, a pledge" (see **truth**). It is attested from 1560s as "contract to give (a woman) in marriage to another, affiance." Related: **Betrothed**; *betrothing*.

covenant (n.)
c. 1300, *covenaunt*, "mutual compact to do or not do something, a contract," from Old French *covenant, convenant* "agreement, pact, promise" (12c.), originally present participle of *covenir* "agree, meet," from Latin *convenire* "come together, unite; be suitable, agree," from *com-* "together" (see **com-**) + *venire* "to come," from a suffixed form of PIE root ***gwa-** "to go, come."
In law, "a promise made by deed" (late 14c.). Applied in Scripture to God's arrangements with man as a translation of Latin *testamentum*, Greek *diatheke*, both rendering Hebrew *berith* (though *testament* also is used for the same word in various places). Meaning "solemn agreement between members of a church" is from 1630s; specifically those of the Scottish Presbyterians in 1638 and 1643 (see **covenanter**).

*gwa-

*gwā-, also **gwem-*, Proto-Indo-European root meaning "to go, come."
It forms all or part of: **acrobat**; **adiabatic**; **advent**; **adventitious**; **adventure**; **amphisbaena**; **anabasis**; **avenue**; **base** (n.) "bottom of anything;" **basis**; **become**; **circumvent**; **come**; **contravene**; **convene**; **convenient**; **convent**;

conventicle; **convention**; **coven**; **covenant**; **diabetes**; **ecbatic**; **event**; **eventual**; **hyperbaton**; **hypnobate**; **intervene**; **intervenient**; **intervention**; **invent**; **invention**; **inventory**; **juggernaut**; **katabatic**; **misadventure**; **parvenu**; **prevenient**; **prevent**; **provenance**; **provenience**; **revenant**; **revenue**; **souvenir**; **subvention**; **supervene**; **venire**; **venue**; **welcome**.
It is the hypothetical source of/evidence for its existence is provided by: Sanskrit *gamati* "he goes," Avestan *jamaiti* "goes," Tocharian *kakmu* "come," Lithuanian *gemu, gimti* "to be born," Greek *bainein* "to go, walk, step," Latin *venire* "to come," Old English *cuman* "come, approach," German *kommen*, Gothic *qiman*.

pact (n.)

"an agreement between persons or parties," early 15c., from Old French *pacte* "agreement, treaty, compact" (14c.) and directly from Latin *pactum* "agreement, contract, covenant," noun use of neuter past participle of *pacisci* "to covenant, to agree, make a treaty," from PIE root ***pag-** "to fasten." Related: *Paction* "act of making a pact."

*pag-

also **pak-*, Proto-Indo-European root meaning "to fasten."
It forms all or part of: **Areopagus**; **appease**; **appeasement**; **compact** (adj.) "concentrated;" **compact** (n.1) "agreement;" **fang**; **impact**; **impale**; **impinge**; **newfangled**; **pace** (prep.) "with the leave of;" **pacific**; **pacify**; **pact**; **pagan**; **page** (n.1) "sheet of paper;" **pageant**; **pale** (n.) "limit, boundary, restriction;" **palette**; **palisade**; **patio**; **pawl**; **pax**; **pay**; **peace**; **peasant**; **pectin**; **peel** (n.2) "shovel-shaped instrument;" **pole** (n.1) "stake;" **propagate**; **propagation**; **travail**; **travel**.
It is the hypothetical source of/evidence for its existence is provided by: Sanskrit *pasa-* "cord, rope," *pajra-* "solid, firm;" Avestan *pas-* "to fetter;" Greek *pegnynai* "to fix, make firm, fast or solid," *pagos* "pinnacle, cliff, rocky hill;" Latin *pangere* "to fix, to fasten," *pagina* "column," *pagus* "district;" Slavonic *paž* "wooden partition;" Old English *fegan* "to join," *fon* "to catch seize."

Tell me the truth! Why did they lie to me? Because none of us really can handle the truth! Truth is an agreement! Truth is a covenant! A pact! You agreed to agree! A document and you signed your name to it!

agreement (n.)

c. 1400, "mutual understanding" (among persons), also (of things) "mutual conformity," from Old French *agrement, agreement*, noun of action from *agreer* "to please" (see **agree**). Attested in English by early 15c. as "formal or documentary agreement, terms of settlement."

There is no such thing as ONE version of truth. Many types of truth.

Perspective based Truth
Coherentism means the truth is coherent or matches what's in your head
Pragmatism means the the truth is useful to you in some way, so you accept it

Correspondence Theory (based on reality, corresponds with something real)
Math
Geometry

Removal Theory
Deflationism says take truth out to the conversation... it is what it is
Nihilism says truth does not even exist and ignores its existence

Clear truths exist! (No logical debate exists)
You are here! You exist!
And mathematical equations like $1+1=2$

Other truths
Truths of reasoning (analysis)
Truths of Fact (experience)
Objective truths (laws of the Universe whether you believe them or not, gravity for ex)
Personal truths (true to you due to your experience)
MY PERSONAL TRUTH IS NOT THE SAME AS YOURS ITS TRUE TO ME
WE GO TO WAR OVER PERSONAL TRUTHS due to being sealed off from arguments of reason, not open to CONVERSATION
Political Truth (statements repeated until in your subconscious, programming)

You can deny truth of fact because not everyone has the same experience or outcome, but you cannot deny, although you may choose to, truths of reason because there are receipts for the truth ie cold hard evidence! How did you arrive at the truth?

Do you have cold hard evidence or is it based off your experience which can differ from person to person? This is called YOUR truth, but it is not THE TRUTH!

TRUTH IS RELATIVE.

relative (adj.)
early 15c., *relatif*, "having reference (to something), relating, depending upon," from Old French *relatif* and directly from Late Latin *relativus* "having reference or relation," from Latin *relatus*, used as past participle of *referre* "bring back, bear back" (see **refer**), from *re-* "back, again" + *lātus* "borne, carried" (see **oblate** (n.)).
Meaning "having mutual relationship, connected with each other" is from 1590s; that of "arising from or determined by relationship to something else" is from 1610s; that of "having or standing in a relation to something else" is from 1650s; that of "not absolute or existing by itself" is by 1704. In grammar, "referring to an antecedent," from 1520s.

Truth is relative. relatable. Familiar. It's like family. It's blood. And when it doesn't feel familiar to us, we label it a lie. Why? Because it doesn't match our reality. It does not feel UNIVERSAL.

Universe

from PIE root ***wer-** (2) "to turn, bend." The metaphor is of plowing, of "turning" from one line to another (*vertere* = "to turn") as a plowman does.

The primary purpose of plowing is **to turn over the upper layer of the soil, bringing fresh nutrients to the surface, while burying weeds and the remains of previous crops, allowing them to break down**.

universe (n.)

1580s, "the whole world, cosmos, the totality of existing things," from Old French *univers* (12c.), from Latin *universum* "all things, everybody, all people, the whole world," noun use of neuter of adjective *universus* "all together, all in one, whole, entire, relating to all," literally "turned into one," from *unus* "one" (from PIE root ***oi-no-** "one, unique") + *versus*, past participle of *vertere* "to turn, turn back, be turned; convert, transform, translate; be changed" (from PIE root ***wer-** (2) "to turn, bend").

The English New Testament first was divided fully into verses in the Geneva version (1550s). Meaning "metrical composition" is recorded from c. 1300; as the non-repeating part of a modern song (between repetitions of the *chorus*) by 1918.

The Black people say that in form their old songs usually consist in what they call "Chorus and Verses." The "chorus," a melodic refrain sung by all, opens the song; then follows a verse sung as a solo, in free recitative; the chorus is repeated; then another verse; chorus again;—and so on until the chorus, sung for the last time, ends the song. [Natalie Curtis-Burlin, "Negro Folk-Songs," 1918]

So how Can we know what is really true? In an entity called Monads. While individual, all of our minds are connected to one another though the Universe. The Most High designed it this way. This is why we feel relief when we hear truth and feel weird when someone is lying. It can literally be felt because we are all connected and the connection is severed with a lie... it's like a glitch in the matrix, you saw something is out of alignment with the Universe because it is. UNI- Verse is One song, one sound

Numerology of Truth

Truth 2,9,3,2,8= 24/6   Truth Chaldean 4, 2, 6, 4, 5= 21/3.... 6+3=9

Truth is Creativity, beauty, and responsibility (24/6)
Jupiter it wants to expand and go higher thoughts wisdom beliefs don't stay stuck (21/3)
Venus (24/6) it wants to compartmentalize, likes and dislikes, this is experience, it's relational and speaks of relation to self and others and also how you build and what materials do you build with determines the kind and quality of truth you have!

Mars (9) take action make things happen
Pluto (9) transform and transmute

Truth does not become truth to us until it becomes one with us. Until it creates multiple verses and a chorus in us that repeats over and over, until it becomes a song.

Something does not become a personal truth to us until it has been plowed, dug up and turned over in us... we literally go to war over personal truth just like the plow disturbs hard unyielding ground, objective and political truths disturb our personal truths and we fight to maintain what we deem as truth personally. Be mindful of what you hear, who you are hearing it from, and how often you hear it because if you hear it enough, it will become your personal truth and you will go to war over it when it wasn't even your personal truth to begin with!

WINNING FORMULA FOR RECOGNIZING TRUTH

Stay Objective (be mindful of personal beliefs)
It's not a lie because it's not YOUR experience!
Realize most truths are established thru our conditioning
Analyze it (where did this come from)
Familia is truth! One verse one sound!

PEARL OF WISDOM AND POWER MOMENT

Photo courtesy of Pexels.com by Jessika Arraes

"THE OFFERING"

The way the world is today makes it easy to show just one side of the picture. You can do business with a person you may never meet in person. Offers can seem valuable when you can't see clearly. This requires patience on your part. Don't be so quick to take an offering or what may look like a door of opportunity. Truth is relative to the person with the experience. No two people have had the EXACT same experience, so their truths will vary and that's ok. When someone offers you a truth, it's their truth. It does not become your truth until you have sat with it and make it your own based on your experience.

NOTE TO THE READER

My hope is that you have enjoyed the short, selected lessons from the first full year of the Pearls of Wisdom and Power.

I hope that you can take the lessons, the winning formulas, and the pearl of wisdom and power moments and use them to strengthen yourself, build up your courage and confidence and change the trajectory of your life for the better.

Currently, you can listen to the show on the Clubhouse app under the Pearls of Wisdom and Power clubhouse room. Some of the shows are also uploaded to Apple Podcasts, Google Podcasts, Spotify, Anchor.fm, and soon to be YouTube.

If you are looking for a spiritual mentor or spiritual coach with a sound mind and safe spiritual practices, look no further. You may schedule a clarity session or reading with me via my website under schedule a consultation:

https://dornorconsulting.services

Or you can follow me on Instagram under @dornorconsulting and click the linktree link in the bio to schedule a clarity session, astrology reading, numerology reading or one of the many other offerings I offer.

I look forward to helping you with your ascension!

Love y'all,

Michelle 🧑🏾 ♏

ABOUT THE AUTHOR

Michelle Dornor, is the author of 3 publications to date titled, *She Her Hers: Inspiration for the Enlightened Women's Soul;The Blackness In Me: Poetic Life Lessons from Cleveland to Accra*; and her latest work, *Pearls of Wisdom and Power: Life Changing Lessons for Spiritual Advancement.*

Michelle is the proud Owner and Founder of Dornor Consulting LLC which is a consulting firm that assists others to discover, develop, gain clarity on, and transform their personal and professional lives.

Michelle is a Summa Cum Laude and Honors Fellow graduate of Ashford University with a double major Bachelor of Arts in Public Relations and Marketing.

She is a current member of several honor societies to include Golden Key International Honor Society, Sigma Beta Delta, Alpha Sigma Lambda, and SALUTE Veterans National Honor Society.

Michelle hosts a weekly Tuesday Inspiration online talk show called Pearls of Wisdom and Power. She is also a licensed minister in the prophetic realm and is a member of WYO POETS which is a local poetry group that meets monthly and performs spoken word and various poetic prose for the local community.

Michelle proudly served her country as a United States Air Force military member during Desert Storm and Desert Shield. She currently works as a Sales Professional for a Fortune 500 Tech company for the past 12 years and has more then 30 years of experience in sales and customer service.

Contact for Inquiries

For general inquiries or to book her for a speaking engagement: You may contact her at:

dornorconsulting@gmail.com
https://dornorconsulting.services

OTHER BOOKS BY THE AUTHOR

The Blackness in Me: Lessons of Life from Cleveland to Accra is a collection of 23 pieces of intimate poetry about the author's personal experience while being Black in America and abroad.

Written from the divine feminine perspective, it contains prose that will make you laugh, make you cry, and get you stirred to action. The celebration and history of Juneteenth was in mind as Michelle collected memories of her life as an adolescent to adulthood. There is something here for everyone to enjoy. With the stroke of her pen, Michelle weaves a wonderful tapestry of a collection that is heart wrenching at times, but also a beautiful journey through the lens of an African American woman in America who one day stepped foot on our ancestor's land in Accra, Ghana, West Africa.

Available on Amazon, Barnes & Noble, and anywhere books are sold global wide.

She Her Hers: Inspiration for the Enlightened Woman's Soul, her first major publication. It is a special Mother's Day 2021 edition. Designed for the spiritually awake woman from all walks of life. It contains 18 full length poems and prose to bliss the divine feminine within. Within, you will find musings about all the women and the roles they play. Her hope is that you will find inspiration, love, peace, and joy within these pages.

Available on Amazon in paperback or ebook.